Bill
of
Bulwell

By Bill Cross

British Library Cataloguing in Publication Data
A catalogue record for this book is available from the British Library

ISBN 0 9516960 5 X

PLOWRIGHT PRESS
P O BOX 66
WARWICK CV34 4XE

Orders by direct mail or through a bookseller

£6.95 (post free UK)

Cover design: 3rd Millenium, Wellesbourne House, Wellesbourne
Printer: Warwick Printing Co., Warwick

TO PAMELA

CONTENTS   Page

PART 2: PAID WORK BEGINS

PART 3: WARTIME

PART 4: SETTLING DOWN

PART 5: MINER

PART 6: ADAPT AGAIN

Cover photo: The complete team needed for one shift of shaft sinking at Calverton. Bill shown on right hand of bottom row

Some years ago, I became a community historian because my work left me dissatisfied at the way 'ordinary' people's lives are often rendered invisible in social policy and in history.

Individual voices need to be heard. It is the experiences of 'ordinary' people which give valuable clues to the way society functions. Their stories are not constructed to fit academic theories. And unlike so many official reports about local communties their stories testify that people with shared or similar backgrounds cannot be stereotyped.

'Ordinary' people tell their stories the way they remember them. Bill explained that he was little schooled in grammar and spelling. In editing Bill's story, I have sorted out the grammar and the spelling enough to make clear copy, but I have left his style in tact because it is his and it makes a good read.

His story tells of the making of a working man and his experiences over a lifetime. Readers are made very aware of how, at the time, much of his life seemed pre-determined by events outside his control, and yet he kept a strong sense of his own identity which, as a pensioner, he still enjoys. He gives readers an unselfconscious historical insight into issues of family life, gender, work and recreation.

Bill's story is written from memory not from diaries or research. Of the truth of its substance, he has not a flicker of doubt. He feels that people are sometimes 'corrected' too harshly over an occasional slight difference of date or emphasis which does not alter the essential truth of their stories.

Bill of Bulwell is the first of a new series.

Ruth I Johns   September 1995

i

*Bill and Joan on their
wedding day: 1948*

INTRODUCTION

Have you ever thought why you were born in a certain town? It is through past relatives. I was born in Bulwell, Nottingham, and here is why. In the years around 1880, my Grandfather was a farm labourer in Hitchin, in Hertfordshire, where he married my Grandmother, a maid servant. By this time, the Industrial Revolution had begun. In Nottingham, coal mines were being sunk and railways being built.

Farm labourers wages were very poor. So hundreds of people left the land and travelled to these new industrial jobs for a better living. That is why my Grandparents on my Mother's side came here. They had a large family which was expected in those days. When their children grew up and married, they all lived within walking distance.

Grandma died while I was quite young. But Grandad lived to a long age of 86 years. Every six months, in his retirement on a few shillings pension, he moved to live with a different daughter. I can still remember his country accent when he lived with us when I was a child. He would say: "Sit you down" or "Your Mother will be coming directly."

My other Grandparents were born in Basford, Nottingham. They were a close family, but we never mixed with them or were close. They also had a large family. Some worked in the brick yards, and clay pits, for brick making. I never knew my Grandmother and I met my Grandad only once. My Father told me Grandad died aged 85 years. He was working at the brick works and the family received his week's wages after he died.

I should have liked to know more about my past relatives. I have written the story of events in my life, for future relatives to know what part I played in this now fast moving world.

So, if you can find time to write or record on a cassette the main events of your life, it will fascinate your children and grandchildren in years to come. We are in the computer age of electronics. But still the finest computer is the human brain. But why is it, I can remember things which happened years ago, but I forget to post a letter in my pocket when I go shopping?

I was born on August 13th, 1918, just before the terrible slaughter of young men finished in November. My first recollection was four years later, in 1922. I was lying covered by a heavy coat on a sofa: a long old-fashioned couch coated with dimpled hard oil cloth and stuffed with horse hair. I was looking straight into a roaring coal fire in a black lead polished grate. There was a paraffin lamp for light. The walls were whitewashed. The mantlepiece above the fire was covered with dark green velvet. Silk tassles hung down. On each end was a pot dog, in the centre a mirror.

The floor was covered in red quarry tiles. There was a brass fender on a whitewashed hearth with fire irons, a rake, a poker, a dustpan and a small tin ladle to scoop water from the boiler heated by the fire. A large black kettle was singing as steam came out of the spout. The fender stopped the hot coals falling on the home-pegged rug near the fire. In the centre of the room was a bare pine table covered in a newspaper table cloth.

Mother stood near the door, wide open as she fed bread to the fowls in the back garden. Her long hair hung down in a plait over the shawl on her shoulders. Sometimes a fowl would wander in to pick crumbs from under the table. As I grew older, I asked my Mother about this memory. She was amazed as it was true. I had been ill with measles. My next memory was holding my Mother's hand going to school on my first day, aged five.

Bulwell used to be a small town on the outskirts of Nottingham noted for its lace and Robin Hood. It was set in a valley. The

2

River Leen flows through Bulwell. The legend is that a bull ran with its horns into the sandstone face. This started a trickle of water from the stone which formed a well, thus Bulwell.

The river starts around Newstead Village, Lord Byron country. There used to be water mills along the river: Forge Mill, Bulwell Mills, Bobbers Mill. All worked by the power of the river, with bleaching and dying of cloth taking place at the riverside.

Bulwell was also rich in minerals: coal, stone for lime making, clay for brick making and clay plant pots. In the stone wall of the Coopers Arms, a large stone engraved by a mason's chisel in large letters said The Lime Kiln Inn. I asked the old landlord about the sign. He said it was dated 1830 when it was built but the old name had been changed before his time. I was still interested so I asked the old quarrymen.

Sometimes people would say: "Do you live up Kill Yards?" It was a nickname. Then I was told it was known as Kiln Yards. Before cement was made, all building was done with mortar, sand and lime mixed. The sandstone or limestone was burnt to a powder in kilns, in the quarries. This lime mortar was used to build stone walls and houses. It must have been good. It lasted hundreds of years in buildings still here.

To the north of Bulwell more quarries were dug for clay, for making bricks in brick kilns and Sankeys clay plant pots were spun by hand and sent all over the world. Even the Royals used them in their nurseries.

I had often seen men and boys with their clothes stained red by making pots from clay. You could buy a plant pot with a domed lid with a slot in it for a money box. When it was full, you just broke it open.

Quite near my garden, a quarry, Culleys, was still working supplying rockery stone. I often heard the blasting on my walks. The men would be seen sitting down with hammer and chisel dressing the stone lumps into shape for the mason. Even from my garden at some time stone had been taken.

As I was digging, there were lots of parts of clay pipes in the soil. One day I found a brass disc. It had a name and number on. I showed it to an old quarry man. He told me some quarry owners also owned village stores. They paid their workers part of their wages in these disks so they had to use their village shop to buy food.

Bill Cross   November 1994

FAMILY TREE.

ARTHUR COPSE · ELIZABETH · MARKHAM — WILLIAM CROSS · MARY SMITH

1857 TO 1943   1860 TO 1922.   1850 TO 1935   1855 - 1918

MARRIED 1878   MARRIED 1875

SONS	DAUGHTERS	SONS	DAUGHTERS
THOMAS	KATE	WILLIAM	ELIZABETH
ARCHIBALD	CLARA	ALFRED	EMMA
WILLIAM	FANNY	THOMAS	POLLY
ALFRED	CHARLOTTE	GEORGE	AIDA
EDWARD			ETHEL
			EADY.

CHARLOTTE COPSE   MARRIED 1904   GEORGE CROSS.
1880 TO 1964   1876 TO 1960

SONS.   DAUGHTER

THOMAS CROSS	GEORGE CROSS	WILLIAM CROSS	MARY CROSS.
1909 TO 1990	1916 TO 1982	1918 —	1921 —
MARRIED	MARRIED	MARRIED	MARRIED
MABEL KEETLY	DORETHY SMITH.	JOAN ALMA BRAND	GEORGE LEE.
1938	1947	1948	1940

DAUGHTER, AUDREY CROSS 1939 —	SON.. DAUGHTERS MELVIN, JOAN GEFFREY. BILL HAD FITHTEEN CHILDREN LOST TOUCH WITH FAMILY	DAUGHTER PAMELA CROSS. 14·2·53 MARRIED BRYN HOWE 1973.	SON VICTOR LEE	DAUGHTER VERONICA LEE LOST TOUCH WITH FAMILY.

MARRIED MICHAL TAYLOR. 1959.

SONS	DAUGHTER		DAUGHTERS
ALLEW TAYLOR	FIONA SALLY TAYLOR		REBECCA 23-7-79 } HOWE LORNA JANE 22-9-83

5

PART 1

CHILDHOOD

THE USEFUL ROOM

The kitchen was the dining room, lounge and general do-it-yourself room, including bathroom. Dad even repaired boots on a cobbler's iron on the kitchen table. In one corner was a Singer sewing machine. By the light of a candle, Mother, with her feet on the treadle, would alter clothes from the eldest to fit the next one down.

The bare pine table was set all day: newspaper table cloth on, paraffin lamp in the centre, teapot, sugar bowl, thick condensed milk tin with its lid open, a large carving knife to cut the homemade bread.

Sometimes if we kids were hungry, we would cut ourselves a slice of bread spread with the thick milk. At one end, the table had remedies for all ailments: senna pods, cod liver oil, rue tea, Friars Balsam, syrup of figs and the dreaded castor oil.

Always above the table was a long sticky fly paper hanging down. We would watch the flies struggle to get free, only to drop sometimes on to food on the table. There was no water tap in the house, or sink. A large bowl for washing the pots stood on the table filled from the black kettle, or ladled from the boiler near the fire.

Babies were bathed in the bowl; clean nappies put on from old pieces of sheets. Using the bowl, Dad washed and shaved with a cut throat razor to cut his whiskers off. All the waste water was carried to the grating outside.

I don't know why but most men at sometime had large abcesses called boils, mostly on their necks. These large inflamed lumps were very painful. A piece of old sheet was laid out on the table, filled with slices of bread, rolled up like a small scarf, dipped in boiling water and put straight on the boil. I heard Dad scream with pain. Known as the bread poultice, this treatment fetched the centre 'core' out.

Crickets lived in the cracks of a small brick wall where the mortar had fallen out each side of the fireplace. They chirped away all day. To stop the noise, we kids stuffed paper in the holes. Small silver fish dashed around the warm hearth.

After coming down stairs and lighting the oil lamp on dark mornings, cockcroaches would scurry off the walls to hide behind the skirting boards. At night, Dad would put out saucers of beer. The black beetles would fall in as they drank and then drown.

It was not because the house was dirty. It was kept very clean with scrubbing and cleaning every day using carbolic soap. I suppose it was the way houses were built. No plaster boards in those days. The thick stone walls were covered in straw, mixed with mortar.

Out of the back door was a communal yard paved with dark blue bricks. Clothes lines stretched from every house. There were six houses and each house picked a day to wash.

The pine table was scrubbed clean every day. From under it a drawer pulled out, filled with knives, forks, spoons and the dreaded cane. It was an old violin bow with its lost string. When the drawer was pulled out, the knives etc made a rattle. If we misbehaved, the drawer was pulled out with a rattle, and a tap on the legs with the cane came. It puzzled us kids why, when we opened the drawer for a knife and fork - making a rattle - the dog crawled under the sofa. Then we realised, he too had tasted the dreaded cane!

On getting out of bed when we were kids, first thing Mother did was pull the bedclothes off the bed - she had to be quick - looking for fleas. Sometimes she caught one, brown, on the pure white

8

sheets. Catching it between her thumb nails, she would squash it. Because fleas were hard, then the blood would run down her nails. They must have been in the walls or mattress because all the linen was boiled white.

Just think how lucky we are now with modern clean houses. Then, the coal fire never went out. At night it was called raking up. An old boot was filled with wet coal dust and it burnt slowly all night. Or potatoe peelings were covered with coal slack to burn slowly.

Next morning, poked up again, the fire would soon get hot. This meant the large black kettle and the boiler near the fire kept hot.

Sitting on the home-pegged rug, in front of the warm coal fire, us kids watched Mother at the old pine table. On it was a large earthenware bowl called a pancheon. She was mixing a Christmas cake. When it was mixed, she passed the wooden spoon for us to lick clean.

When it was in the baking tin ready for the oven, she put the pancheon on the rug. We ate the sweet creamy dough, cleaning the bowl out with our fingers. Even the dog had a lick.

Next day the Christmas puddings were mixed. The old black oven stoked up with coals cooked the large cake. When cool, it was trimmed around the edge with Christmas paper and a Father Christmas put on top. But the puddings had to be boiled for five or six hours, so the copper boiler we used for washdays was stoked up outside.

As Christmas neared, the door flew open. Father, in his cap, sleeves rolled up, brought in a very large cockerel. It was still in its death throws, wings flapping. As he put it on the peg rug, we kids moved away screaming. Then he came in with the tin bath and put it on the rug.

Putting the dead bird in the bath, he said: "Come on, get plucking."

Feathers were soon flying up to the ceiling. When plucking was finished, he singed all the hairs off the cockerel with lit newspaper whilst holding it by the legs. It was then hung in the coal house.

Next night, in front of the fire again, Mother mixed some flour and water to make a paste. Cutting strips of coloured paper, she showed us how to make paper chains, hanging them over the pictures to trim up for Christmas. The morning arrived. Christmas!

We woke early. In our socks, a shiny new penny, a red apple, an orange, a few nuts, two sugar mice with tails of string, and, for all of us to play with, a blow football game. A goal at each end of the table, we blew the ball till we scored. But the cardboard tubes we blew down went soft with the saliva from our mouths,

The dinner with the cockerel, and Christmas pudding and custard was the best of the year.

SCHOOLDAYS

The large doors into the old Victorian school, along a passageway, classrooms each side, our shoes making a clatter on the wood block floor. The Headmistress came to us, my Mother told her my name and left. The Headmistress tied a coloured thread on my lunch parcel. I noticed all the other parcels in the hamper had one.

"Remember your colour to get the right parcel at lunch time," I was told.

The teacher in the classroom gave us all a piece of cloth, about the size of a handkerchief, showing us how to pull the threads out, rolling them into balls of cotton. A bell was rung for playtime, lunch, then crayons to scribble, on to the next bell, then Mother came to fetch me home.

My school was a short walk from home by a narrow path at the side of the railway. Shoes and socks must be worn. In the streets, we played in bare feet to save our boots for school.

For an old halfpenny, you could buy a strip of licorice about a yard long from a small sweet shop near the school. Or kali sucker or anniseed balls - but you were lucky to get ANY money.

If you were eating an apple, eager eyes watched you. "Save us the core," they would say. The noise and the shouting in the playground was struck silent by the sound of the school bell. We were marched by very strict teachers, like little soldiers, to assemble for prayers.

Most teachers were men, back from the Great War. Very strict discipline taught us to behave. Being late for school was marked on your backside by the Head of the school: three strokes with the cane. Strict control was achieved in the classroom with the leather strap: a leather handle with three prongs of leather. If you did wrong, you were in front of the class with your sleeves rolled up holding out your left hand (so you could write with your right hand). The strap came down heavy on your palm, but the prongs often came up your arm making red wheals. You remembered all day you had done wrong.

At home you kept it a secret, or Dad would want to know what you had been doing, and perhaps then add another clout. I have never forgotten the day I received six strokes. We were doing exams. We sat two at a desk. The boy next to me spoke. I leaned over to answer him. The teacher saw me. I went to the front, rolled both sleeves up for six strokes, three on each hand.

THE LEATHER STRAP

Bill's sketch of his classroom.

"I will not have copying or cheating in my class," said teacher. "Go back to your desk."

I pulled down my sleeves and rubbed my hands to take the sting out. It taught me in future to pay attention to the teacher. Kids

13

used to say rub raw onion into your palm to take the sting out. Others lowered their hand as the strap came down to take the force off the strap. Now seventy years on, I still think discipline and punishment in school, and in the Army, did me more good than harm.

One day I had a fever. Mother kept me from school. I was put in her bed, a large cast iron one with brass knobs on the bed ends. To keep me quiet, she emptied family birthday cards on to the bed. Also photos of family members, some letters with black edges around (these were letters of sympathy I realise now).

As I lay on that feather bed, there was the smell of lavender from tiny bags among the cards, and also the smell of camphor balls when she opened the wardrobe. These kept moths off the clothes.

The railway was at the bottom of the garden. Trains passed by day and night. The house shook as the coal trucks, from the pits, passed by. But we were born to the noise. Looking across the railway was a lush green meadow with the River Leen running through it. Horses in the fields were disturbed by the trains.

Next door, Uncle Bill (my Mother's brother) kept pigeons. I fell asleep with them coo-cooing and the twittering of sparrows in the ivy. Taking old fashioned remedies, castor oil and cod liver oil, I soon recovered. The hot oven iron shelf was wrapped in a blanket to keep me warm.

Monday was our wash day. So, before Dad went to work he filled the bricked-in copper with buckets of water and lit a fire under it. By the time we went to school, Mother had pulled the iron mangle, with its wooden rollers to squeeze the water out of the clothes, on to the yard. Also the dolly tub. It had been a large barrel but had the top half sawn off to make a tub. Boiling water was poured in and shredded soap stirred in.

To knock the dirt out of the clothes, a ponch was used. It was a round piece of beech wood, with a shaft and handle to lift it up and down on to the wet clothes. Then they were threaded through the large beech rollers of the mangle, the water running back into the tub.

Then they went on to the lines across the yard. But all articles of white linen were put to boil in the copper with a touch of dolly blue to bring out the white.

As we arrived from school for dinner, you could see the copper chimney belching out smoke like a tug boat going down the river. Turning the large wheel of the mangle was Mother, Dad's cap on, a shawl on her shoulders, her long hair rolled into a bun on her neck and, in the cold wind, a dew drop on her nose.

As she saw us coming round the corner, she would shout: "Nine ponches each before your dinner." It took me all my time to lift the heavy ponch and to let it drop on the clothes. Dinner was Bubble and Squeak: potatoes and cabbage fried up from Sunday. Before we went back to school, each had a job: wash the pots, scrub the brick tiled floor, fill the paraffin lamp, trim the wick and clean the smoked-up glass chimney, fill the coal bucket.

On wash day, Mother tied round her waist a coarse apron made from a sugar sack.

As we said "Cheerio", she would say: "Come here first."

Holding our neck, she would rub our face with the wet apron. It was like sandpaper and your face stung all the way to school.

Coming home at teatime, Mother had finished outside. But the kitchen was full of steam, lines across the ceiling hung with wet clothes. The coal fire was bursting with heat, making the house a sauna. As you sat having your tea, drip, drip, drip down your neck from the wet clothes.

The next day after tea, there were solid lumps of iron being heated up for ironing. The table was cleared for the ironing. As one iron cooled, another was ready. Holding a thick cloth, Mother would take the iron off the fire, turn it to her face, spit on it and if the spit rolled off, it was hot enough. Sometimes you could see the sweat drop of Mother's chin.

We kids sat on the rug in front of the fire. Dad used to say that if a black leaf like a shadow hung on the fire bars that's a sign of a visitor. And, sure enough, a relative would call! Then he would tell us to gaze into the back of the hot coals. After a while, you would see pictures of country scenes and cottages.

The ironing took all night. The shirt collars and cuffs were dipped in Coleman's starch to make them stiff. Next day, all the clothes had to be folded away and aired. Washday could be a three day job, and very tiring work with a large family.

I often wondered why I hated Mondays, but it must have been this experience of Monday miseries of washday. Now to-day, I can get it done within an hour: if only there was a video of those days.
Now I shall have to go, the machine has stopped. The washing is done!

NEVER GOING TO BE A MINER OR SOLDIER!

One dinner time, I was getting ready to go back to school. An old man, as I thought, was selling cottons and lace door to door. Around his neck, held by a string, was a tray of his wares to sell. On his chest was a row of medals. One empty sleeve was tucked in his pocket. He looked a miserable down-and-out. He was a young man who had fought in the war.

Mother bought cottons for her sewing machine. As he turned to go she told him to go and sit under the washhouse roof and she would bring him a mug of tea. She also took two chunks of bread and lard. I remember her words about there was supposed to be a country fit for heroes to live in when they came back from the war. Some MP had promised that, but these men who, by a miracle had survived, were not wanted now.

Thousands were on the dole, a few shillings a week. Yet millions of pounds could be spent on destruction. The poverty, poor living conditions, pitiful wages were everywhere. We were the richest country in the world with a vast empire and we had won the war, But the soldier and the miner were looked down on as the scum of the earth.

I was only very young, but after what I had seen in my childhood, I vowed I would never be a soldier or a miner.

Miners started work about 6.0 a.m. You could hear their heavy boots, on the cobble streets. They had to go over the bridge to the pit at Cinderhill. They wore soft caps, a muffler around their neck. On their belts hung a water bottle. They had a snap tin with their bread and lard in (it was put in a tin because if it was wrapped in paper the mice in the mine would get it).

When we were off school, we played by the bridge. By nine o'clock, a lot of miners were on their way back home. At the pit, a few were selected to work and the rest sent home. No work - no pay. As they came back over the bridge, emptying their water bottles, they would give us their bread and lard out of their snap tins.

Miners were looked down upon. To be a soldier was usually the last chance if you could not get work. In war they were heroes. In peace, they were nothing.

The miner was given a pitiful wage for a dangerous job. No safety helmet or boots, or rules. He worked in the clothes he went to work in, and came home in the pit dust to bath in the tin bath. If injured or killed, very little compensation was paid. We saw these depressed workers and the depressed soldiers, some maimed for life, struggle to get work and a decent living.

In the General Strike, 1926, miners went on strike for a rise in wages and better conditions, later joined by the railwaymen. Then everyone stopped work. I was eight years old.

My father was a bricklayer. I remember going with him to a meeting, on Bulwell Market. We came home because the police on horseback broke the meeting up.

With truncheons in their hand, they beat the crowd around the head. These men only wanted a living wage. The landowners and lords of the land also owned the pits. The miners went back to work no better off.

During the strike, I went with my jug to the soup kitchens. Railmen made soup in the washhouse copper, to give a meal to people on starvation rations. A jug of soup and a loaf of bread made a meal for the family. The pawnshops thrived. People built up debts at the corner shops during the strike to get food to exist.

UNION BOYS AND TRAMPS

At school, I was a slow learner. I remember when I left school I learned things quicker. My brain became clearer. Things that bored me at school: geography, arithmetic. Now, the days we had art or science, woodwork or metalwork, it was a joy to go to school. I should have learnt a lesson from this.

When I left school, I should have gone into a career in the subjects I liked. The school baths were under the woodwork shop. One morning a week, we were taken there to learn to swim. The teacher was nicknamed Bulldog, a big fat ex-Army type. As we stood in our little shorts along the bath's edge, he bellowed: "Get in and start swimming."

A lot of us scrambled out, frightened. We never did learn to swim. The art teacher was very good. He gave each boy a page out of a magazine to colour. Mine was the gentleman with the monocle on Scotch Whisky. I was top of the class with my drawing put up in the main hall. That year I was top in woodwork and metalwork, and science also.

Breaking up for Christmas holidays, we had an apple, orange, sandwich, lemonade, then to the main hall to watch the school play. It was A Christmas Carol. I really enjoyed it. The ghost effect was done by draping a fine net in front of the cast. I think it's a story every kid should read.

At school some boys were dressed differently, in grey pullovers, short grey trousers and socks, always spotlessly clean. They were called Union Boys, from the Workhouse on Highbury Vale. Most were orphans. Tramps also went to the Workhouse for a meal and a night's sleep.

Outside, there was an acre of land. Next day they had to do some digging to pay for their bed and breakfast.

One day when I came in from school, a man was in the garden talking to Mother.

"This is your Uncle Bill" I was told.

I was named after him. He wore a rough worsted suit, heavy boots and a cap. He had a weatherbeaten face, and striking blue eyes which I also inherited from my Dad's side of the family.

He didn't stay long and that was the last time I saw him. My Dad told me he was a younger brother and he was a tramp. He roamed the country doing gardening, living rough in Summer. Then in the Winter months, he lived in the Workhouse doing work for his bed and board. They gave him a suit and boots.

My Dad said Bill had been in the Navy in the War and could not settle after. The Workshouse was the last resort for some folk.

When I worked at the groceries store, I use to deliver on my bike to very poor families. They had to sign for the groceries. The Parish Council would send them vouchers instead of money for a week's food. This meant at least the family had food on the table. If it had been money, it might have gone on beer or cigs.

Sometimes a tramp would come to the door selling bunches of wild flowers put together in bright colours. They would sit in the meadows bunching them together to make a few pennies. There being no Social Security, people had to make a living the best they could.

One such man went around Bulwell repairing harnesses for horses. His horse pulled an old van which he also lived in. I used to be fascinated by the way he repaired the leather with a bradawl making the holes, and threading twine through. He always had work because most things were horse drawn.

The cobbler did another mending job, sewing shoes by hand but mostly it was studs for boots for hard wearing on the cobbled streets. Today a lot of shoes are thrown away when they could be repaired because people can afford new.

Older folk still remember the struggle. Even now, I keep left overs in the refrigerator when I should throw them away and we are careful on spending, looking at a loaf at say the price of 50p and thinking when one was two old pence. But we can't live in the past!

BARBER'S SHOP

One day Dad took me to have my hair cut in the front room of a house which had once been a front parlour. After my hair was cut, I was given a comic to read while Dad was shaved. As I sat on a stool facing a large mirror on the wall I saw three barber's chairs in a row.

A small boy who had just left school, known as the lather boy, put the towel under a man's chin, then with soap and brush, lathered his face rubbing the soap in hard with his fingers. Then when he had a good lather, he went to the next chair.

Then the demon barber took over. The cut-throat razor is a frightening weapon. On a leather strop, he sharpened the blade. Pulling a hair out of Dad's head and holding it up, he cut it in two with one quick move. With quick strokes, he then took the soap and whiskers off each side of his face.

But I held my breath as he held his chin, taking the razor down his throat and over his Adam's Apple. Then holding his nose, he did around the moustache and chin. After the shave, hot towels were put around his face to soothe the skin. Dad stood up, looked in the mirror.

"That will be tuppence Sir." A frightening experience for a young boy! Thank God for the safety razor!

As we came out of the barber's, it was market day in Bulwell town centre. We had come down a small alley at the side of the Olympia Music Hall (now Woolworths store) on the cobbled stones. By the drinking trough for the horses, a woman was selling hot peas and we stopped for a big bag of chips cooked in a big pan of lard on a large oil drum with holes in and full of burning coke fuel.

Stalls with their striped tops, spread along the market to where the trams turned their poles to go back to Nottingham. We watched the man at one stall. He was called Mad Harry. He was selling watches and chains. Every man wore a waistcoat with a pocket watch and its chain fastened in a button hole.

"Who will give me ten shillings for this fine watch?" he asked.

Nobody answered. When the price dropped to two shillings and nobody was interested, he hit the watch with a mallet and its springs shot out everywhere. Dad said he was mad.

At the Olympia Music Hall I remember the billing outside. Maria Martin in the Red Barn and Charlie Peace. Two murder plays. I begged Dad to take me, so we came back that night. The stalls were lit up by paraffin flares (a tank of paraffin, dripped down, burning on the end of the pipe, like a flare). It was dark and dismal in the theatre. The stage was lit by small paraffin lamps. Maria Martin was about a girl being murdered in a barn. I can remember Charlie Peace jumping out of a railway carriage.

After, Dad bought me a coloured pocket watch, with chain, for half-a-crown (25p) just as Mad Harry was going to hit it with a mallet. I treasured it for years.

In Bulwell in those days life was easy going. Everything was horse drawn or push bike. It was green fields around the outskirts of town. Most people walked for miles because there was only the trams back and forth to Nottingham. And those who had private transport looked for a good horse for a trap which seated four to six people.

1926: YEAR OF THE STRIKE

There was a heat wave. Over the bridge and the fields, we bathed in the River Leen. Bather costumes were unheard of. Girls and boys stripped off. We lay in the rushes to dry. Some days, leaving our clothes we would paddle along the Leen to Bulwell town.

We learned the hard way. After cutting our feet on broken glass in the river, we wore slippers when paddling. Some of us had fishing nets, a jam jar for the sticklebacks or gudgeon we caught.

We paddled under the old stone bridge near the Horse Shoe pub, then under the bridge up to the church. Through there was the large wooden water wheel that drove the mill. This was the best place to catch fish.

Back in the field we would make reed whistles. As we got older there were more exciting games with the girls. One day, a man came to fetch the horses in. He gave us rides on the two Shire Horses. I went with him to the stables just over the river to open the gates.

He was a coal merchant. The two large carts that the horses pulled were near the stables, their shafts pointing to the sky. All tranport was horse drawn. Coal was tipped in the street, to be taken into the house by bucket or by barrow. Everyone relied on a coal fire for warmth and cooking. Milk came to the door in a churn and scooped into a basin. The baker came in horse and van.

The greengrocer had a flat dray. His horse moved slowly along the street as he shouted his wares. Wild rabbits hung on his tailboard. If you bought one, he would hang it on the hook and, with a penknife, skin it in a second.

But he always threw its eyes in the gutter. I didn't like this.

24

On hot Summer nights people sat outside their houses. Some had birdcages on the wall outside with linnets or a bullfinch: wild birds. It was not illegal to keep wild birds or to take their eggs.

People lived close together as a family. Doors were open day and night. If a woman was giving birth, the other children were looked after by neighbours. If someone died, a neighbour would come and wash the victim and lay them out for the burial.

The Tally man cometh! The travelling man with his suitcase would call. Most people had no money to buy from this man: a suit, frock, table linen, bedding. He would call on Friday night for a few shillings toward the debt you owed. Most were never out of debt. But at least this way, things needed could be had. They could never be bought with cash.

You never heard of a burglar because there was nothing to steal and the punishment was severe. Our postman stole a five shilling postal order from a letter and was caught. He was sentenced to six months hard labour, on bread and water to survive. I remember seeing him when he came out: a skeleton of a man. For crimes like rape: the cat of nine tails or birch rod across the back. Those who received this punishment did not offend again. They and their families suffered the shame from the neighbourhood.

From the age of seven or eight, we had to attend Sunday School, over the Bridge to Coventry Road Baptist Church, morning and afternoon. Mother went to church at night with a friend. Once a year, on the Sunday School Anniversary, we had new clothes. We also went on week nights to the Boys Brigade and also did plays on the stage.

We came in from playing in the hot dusty streets with tar on our knees. The summers were very hot and melted the tar on the streets until it ran down in the gutters. Mother rubbed lard on our knees to melt the tar.

In the very cold Winter with snow falls, we made sledges out of crates. One day we found a large door, dragged it to the top of the sloping street and seven or eight of us rode down on it.

To warm our hands we made Winter Warmers: a large tomato tin with the lid cut off. With wire, we made a handle: like a bucket. Then we filled the tin with paper and sticks, lit it and swung it in a circle over our heads to make it burn. There were always plenty of small bits of coal on the streets. We soon had a roaring fire in the tin to warm our hands.

But there would be small accidents. Someone would be hit on the head and his hair caught fire.

There was no radio or television, just the wind-up gramophone with its large green horn to amplify the sound. The lighting in the kitchen by paraffin and candles wasn't very good for reading, so we mostly played under the gas lamps in the street. As it came dusk, the lamplighter with a long pole, a small flame on the end, pushed it up to the lamp and it would light up.

Like all boys, we got into mischief, but never vandalism. There were metal pipes bringing the water from the gutter to the drain on the pavement. We would stuff it with paper from the bottom and light it. It roared up like a rocket. As the people came out to look, we would be gone!

Most houses had front doors at the side of each other and they had large brass knobs. We would tie these together with string, then knock on both doors.

As each neighbour opened his door, it shut the other one making a tug-of-war. We would play under the lamp on the bridge with a whip and top, cigarette cards and SNOBS (four squares of baked clay). Using one hand to throw them up, they were caught on the back of the other hand. Sometimes we would go scrumping, stealing apples. We dare not take them home so we would hide them. On the way to school, we would share them out.

At Christmas time, we would get together to go carol singing and at the end of the evening share the money out. Some of the more well-to-do people would ask you inside. We would be given six pence each and a mince pie. Some joker would put 'hot pennies' on the fireside and, with gloves on, put them in our hands and then shut the door.

The shop in the street sold everything: fish and chips at one end. Also ice cream, sweets, fruit and vegetables, tobacco and reading books and comics.

For a penny, you could buy a large bag of touched fruit and then cut the bad parts out. The rest was edible. Also for a penny, you could buy pot herbs, a carrot, turnip, parsnip, onion, a piece of celery, all for the stew pot to make a meal for seven or eight with home baked bread in the gravy.

BLACKSMITH'S SHOP AND FORGE

As I went regularly to the stables, Ted said: "Now you are off school and used to the horses, can you come early to the stables? I have a lot of coal to deliver and Jelly has to go to the blacksmith to have new shoes on."

This large carthorse was called Jelly because when you went near him, his body quivered. I was at the stables early at seven. The horse was lying down but stood up as I went in, shaking the straw off his back. I was so small I stood on a box to put the bridle on, forceing the bit between his teeth. After walking him out of the stable, I tied the reins to one of the carts, climbed on the cart and dropped on his back. He was quite docile for a big horse.

Taking the reins I walked him slowly along the cobbled streets to Bulwell market, then turned up Commercial Road. At Key Street, the blacksmith was at the side of The Cross Keys pub. As I turned into the street, I felt so proud being in control of a powerful horse. The blacksmith greeted me and, with his powerful hands, lifted me down off Jelly.

The shop was an open shed with a fire being pumped by bellows to get a fierce heat to hot the metal. On the walls hung all the sizes of horse shoes and tools. The smith and his mate were in striped shirts with rolled up sleeves, no collars. Around the waist, he wore a thick leather apron split down between the legs. He told me to sit on a box as he led Jelly into the forge tying him to the side of the fire.

Standing with his back to the horse, the blacksmith lifted his leg between his in the split of the apron. Prising the old shoe off, with a very sharp knife he trimmed the hoof level.

His mate was pumping the bellows, making the fire hot around a strip of metal. I watched as the blacksmith took the white hot bar out of the fire with tongs, shaping it on the anvil into a shoe. The ring of metal echoed with the sound of a steel punch as it made nail holes in the shoe. As it was cooling down, the punch still in the shoe, he lifted the horses leg again between his and put the hot shoe on the hoof to burn in the shape.

Clouds of smoke and acrid smell of burning bones filled the forge. Then there was steam as the shoe was plunged into water. With the horse's leg firmly held between his knees, he put the cold shoe on the hoof.

Using special nails, as they came through the soft hoof, he twisted the points off and, with a rasp, smoothed around the hoof. When the four new shoes were on, he painted them black.

"There you are m'lad," he said as he lifted me back on Jelly and giving me the reins: "off you go."

He gave the horse a slap. With a clatter of new shoes on the granite cobble stones I rode back to the stables. Climbing off on the carts in the stable and standing on a box again, I took the bridle off, put a bucket of oats in the manger and Jelly was soon chomping away. From the box, I gave him a good grooming with curry comb and brush, while whistling to stop the dust going in my throat. Around the backside, I hung on to his tail in case he kicked out.

When Ted came back, he was very pleased, giving me a shilling, a lot of money for a small boy.

A LOAD TO REMEMBER

One day we set off from the stables, with the other horse a big grey mare. She was very powerfully built as she was part Shire. The large two-wheeled cart could hold three or four tons of coal, with side boards to stop the coal spilling out. It was a crisp frosty morning and we went slowly to Linby pit. Bulwell Hall Estate was not built. It was farm land. At the pit top we loaded large lumps of household coal. Coming back to Bulwell was no trouble. The mare pulled the heavy load with ease along the narrow country lanes. But in the market, the steep Church Hill was facing us.

Ted said: "Are you ready Bill. You take her head."

He shouted at the mare to go on. She pulled the load. Sparks flew off her shoes as they hit the granite cobbles.

Using the whip, Ted shouted: "GO ON." At the head I could see the horse was nearly on its knees. Ted came up to me and turned the mare's head, and the heavy load hit the curb, stopping it pulling her down the hill. Clouds of steam came off her body as Ted let her get her second wind. He lit a fag. The cart was now scotched against the kerb.

Ted rubbed her neck saying: "You can do it my beauty." I thought no way can she move the load on the steep hill. After five minutes, he said: "Get to her head, Bill." He shouted and with the whip, she dug her shoes in the granite, sparks flying. The heavy load moved slowly up the hill. Outside the Church, on level ground, the mare was all in. Ted took off his neckerchief to wipe the white foam sweat off the mare.

Ted said to me: "You gave up Bill, I knew she could do it." After half-an-hour, we delivered the load to a house in Palin Street, Hyson Green. To this day, I never forgot this struggle.

AFTER THE STRIKE

As kids, we never realised the poverty after the Strike. There was no dole or social. What you learnt was survival. If I remember right, if you were without any means of support you applied to the Board of Guardians. They would send an inspector to your house. If you had a luxury like a piano, it had to be sold. If you had sons or daughters working, their wages were taken into consideration.

The corner shop was a stand-by. Each customer had a 'book.' If a man was out of work it was called Strap. Every time you purchased in the shop, it would be entered into the book. When in work you paid off the debt so you had it 'on tick.'

The Pawnbroker was a godsend. On a Monday, Dad's suit could go in for ten shillings and would be fetched out on a Saturday for twelve shillings after Dad was paid. He could go out in it on Saturday and Sunday, and it would be back at the pawnbroker on Monday.

All food was home-made, mostly stews even for Sunday breakfast. But we always had a good Sunday dinner, the best meal of the week.

Dad often had 'soaky.' This was a basin of tea with bread broken into it, like soup. Sometimes we had thick condensed milk on home baked bread, spread on like jam. Bread was baked twice a week in the iron oven. I watched the dough rise in the pancheon in front of the fire.

If you were granted help from the Board of Guardians, you did not get cash. You were given food vouchers to spend at the local shop. I think this would be a good idea today because a lot of benefits are spent on beer and cigs: no help to the family.

Frozen food was unknown. The butcher had to sell meat quickly. The carcasses were stored in his cellar covered in ice.

On Saturday night, you could buy meat very cheap because it would not keep fresh. When you brought it home, it was cooked and put on the cool stone slab under the stairs.

Most children had pocket money when their Dads were working: one old penny on Friday night out of his wages. Our spending money too was given us on Friday night when Dad had his wages - one penny each. We would have our noses to the sweet shop window for ages deciding how to spend our fortune.

SUNDAY DINNER

Over the railway bridge, Dad had a large garden. We kids were taught to dig and sow. Besides the few fowls around the house, Dad's favourite hobby was breeding rabbits. The largest you have ever seen were called Belgian hares.

We would take a sack along the country lanes picking wild parsley and dandelions to fatten them. Also Mam would boil potato peelings which were mashed with bran and made into balls to feed the rabbits in Winter.

On Sunday for dinner, we sat around the pine table with a white linen cloth on instead of newspaper.

From the oven at the side of the roaring fire, Mother lifted a large meat tray placing it on a board on the table. Eager eyes looked in. The largest rabbit lay with its legs up, its stomach filled with stuffing and around its body golden baked potatoes and parsnips. Everyone wanted a leg with carrots and onions from the iron saucepans and thick brown gravy. It was the best dinner of the week.

Next from another black saucepan, she lifted a large snowball of white steaming linen tied in a knot on to a tray. She undid the knot, taking the cloth off. The pudding burst open. Out poured blackberry and apples. We had a large spoonful each covered with steaming custard. It finished the dinner off.

Scraping the plates into the dogs dish, it made a meal for him...and so off to Sunday School over the railway bridge.

JOBS IN THE HOUSE

After doing jobs we were each given two pennies for going to the pictures on Saturday. The jobs were chopping sticks to make the fires in the week, fetching paraffin for the lamp and cleaning it, filling the coal bucket, filling the boiler up for hot water, filling the water bucket under the table, gathering rabbit food, and cleaning out the rabbits and feeding them.

We went to the cinema on Highbury Vale. There were long queues of screaming kids handing in their two pennies at the window.

Everyone rushed for the back seat. When the cinema was full, if you were on the front seats your neck ached through looking up. It was silent films. To accompany them was a large lady at the piano. If the villain crept behind the hero, she would thump it to a crescendo and we kids would shout: "Look behind you."

Charlie Chaplin and Buster Keaton were stars. I remember Charlie Chaplin in a film about a circus. One of the horses was sick. He was told to give it a large pill by blowing it into the horse's mouth through a tube. As he was doing this, the horse coughed and he swallowed the pill. This was silent comedy!

One Saturday when I got home from the pictures, Mother was fast asleep in her chair, with a shawl round her. Shadows flickered around the walls from the fire. She looked so peaceful. But, on the table was a large fruit cake, a knife and plates, ready for us coming home.

I cut myself a piece and let her sleep while I was off to play.

FIRST HOLIDAY

I was about nine years old and on school holidays. Friday morning, Mother packed some clothes and some food with some bottles of cold tea (no vacuum flasks) into a wicker case.

My sister, me and my brother (two years older) set off with Mother to visit aunts and uncles at Bramcote near Stapleford. Dad and my older brother Tom were at work.

I realise now it must have been five miles to walk. We went to Cinderhill Crossroads, up Bells Lane. It was all farms and country lanes. No housing estates then. It was a Summer day. We kept sitting on the grass for a rest and drink with a sandwich. But it was tiring for our young legs.

We came to Trowell Canal near Bramcote. As we walked along the tow path, horses pulled barges along. Over small stone bridges, then up a narrow lane, then we ran back under a bridge to shelter from a Summer storm which only lasted a few minutes.

I remember this because all along the lanes afterwards were hundreds of tiny frogs jumping about. They were only about one inch long. You never see this happen today.

We arrived at the farm cottage about tea-time, greeted by Aunt Kate and Uncle Arthur. It stood in acres of fields. There was a low-beamed room, a large open stone fire place with big logs burning. From a big black kettle, she made tea. They had four children and with our three, this made seven. We went to play in the garden and orchard with swings on the apple trees.

They had rabbits in hutches, fowls, geese and ducks. The geese chased us with their long necks stretched. What sticks in my mind: the toilets! In an outbuilding, boards with two holes covered two buckets. You sat at the side of each other. Twin toilets!

At eight, we were called in for a large bowl of soup.

Then, in our night shirts, up the creaking stairs. But there was only one large bed. We slept head to toe like sardines in a tin. I had someone's feet in my face! We stayed until Monday, visiting other relatives. Some uncles had good jobs. We were given half-a-crown, a fortune for a kid.

Then we walked slowly back to Bulwell tired after the long walk.

The market centre was covered with roundabouts driven by steam, and stalls where you could win good prizes like tea services or large teddy bears, clocks, rings and pocket watches. The Fair spread on to the bogs at the side of the Leen, over the old stone bridge to the Horse Shoe Pub.

You could go over the railway crossing up to Highbury Vale, or catch a train to Nottingham. Or go the other way to Annesley, Kirkby, Sutton, through to Mansfield and the north. The trams came across the market to where the Pork Farms shop is now, then turning the poles and the seats to go back to the city.

Along Main Street (or 'up town') was the Palace Cinema, known as the flea pit. It was silent films, but you came out scratching yourself all over.

Back in the cobble stoned centre, there were rides, the steam boat, big horses, cakewalk, the smell of steam, paraffin, coal and coke burning, or home-made toffee. The man put it on a hook, then cut it into squares when it was cool. A penny for a big bag.

The boxing booth at the side of the Horse and Jockey was a big attraction. Outside the show stood a powerful man in trunks.

Another man shouted: "Take on the champion for one round. Win ten shillings."

This was a lot of money then. The boxer was a professional. Some challengers fancied themselves especially after a few drinks. So the crowd poured in to see the fight. Sometimes it only took one blow. Some, by a miracle, stayed the distance.

Ladies wore large hats held on by large hat pins, their long hair rolled into a bun on their necks. They had thin waists, skirts down to the floor covering their button-up boots fastened with a boot hook.

At one stall you could buy chicklings, tripe and boiled pigs feet. You could buy a half-penny worth of chips from the coke brazier, or fresh made brandy snaps, a cock-on-a-stick for a penny, most rides a penny. But when you think that wages then averaged two or three pounds a week, a penny would go a long way.

I remember a runaway horse. I was on Highbury Vale. A horse passed me, its reins trailing, its cart swaying from side to side at terrific speed. The cart turned over pulling the horse down.

A chap sat on its head to hold it down. It had been scared by a firework.

Every day I went over the bridge to the stables. I helped to clean the horses out, and polish brasses on the harness, brush Neatsfoot Oil into the leather. We were going to a horse show. Coloured ribbons were plaited in the manes and tails, muffs with tassles on the ears, hooves painted black and coats brushed to a shine.

As we were doing this, a fellow drove up in a pony and trap. The horse looked neglected, its head hung down. You could see its ribs. After bargaining, Ted bought it. Ted said we would have to feed him up. The horse was cheap because the fellow could not afford to keep it. After a good grooming, his coat looked good. He was a chestnut brown, with four white fetlocks, a white star on the forehead, not a carthorse. We scrubbed the buggy down and painted it a bright green. The wheels had rubber tyres on, the spokes painted bright yellow.

"The bright colours will make them look at us," said Ted.

The door was at the back. You had to put your foot on the iron footstep to enter. It seated six, three each side. The pony soon recovered. Our first ride was on Sunday night into the country with Ted's brother Jack and their Dad. The pony had been trained to pick up its front legs as it trotted along. The first stop was at Cinderhill, The Park Tavern.

A large sign said ALL BEER BREWED ON THE PREMISES. I was left in charge outside while they went in, but Ted bought me a bottle of pop and gave me sixpence.

Near me was another boy with a white pony, the harness decked out with a lot of brasses. Ted came out with some other men. They were dressed in tweed jackets, riding breeches, gaiters and brown boots. As their buggy pulled off, I heard Ted say they were the Roberts Brothers, known as the Forty Thieves of Bulwell for their dodgy deals like Ali Baba. Not long after this, their horse being pure white, I noticed it in our street. I got to know their son George. He was my age and started at my school.

One day he took me to their stables, down Church Lane, now Belmont Avenue. The stables were wood and spread to the Church Yard. I deserted Ted now to go with George. Sometimes we would go on the four-wheeled dray, like a platform on wheels, to the woodpacking department at Players cigarette factory at Radford. We filled huge sacks with clean white sawdust.

When we got back, we put it in small sandbag type bags and tied them up with string. Loading up sometimes as many as two hundred small bags on the dray, we went with his Dad and Uncle to all the pubs and butchers and sold the bags for twopence.

In butchers, sawdust was spread on the floor to soak up blood dripping off meat. It was spread on pub floors.

As well as ponies, Tom and George Roberts also had ferrets and greyhounds. We would go rabbiting and rat clearing. Further down Church Lane were fields. They were swampy with wild watercress growing. We used to ride the ponies there to graze.

Life then was unbelievable, so easy going, the steady pace of the horse and cart, hot dry summers, a penny in your pocket. With half-a-crown you were rich; with a ten shilling note (50p) a millionnaire!

BATH NIGHT: 1930

Every Friday night the roaring fire was surrounded by every saucepan and kettle for boiling water. The pegged-rug was rolled back and the large tin bath filled up in front of the fire and more pans put to boil. There was a bucket of cold water to cool the bath down.

The eldest had the bath first. Then more hot water was added for the next. I remember my turn.

Standing in the bath, I was scrubbed all over with a small brush. Ladles of hot water were poured over my head; then two scoops out of the boiler, very hot. I stepped out like a boiled crab, bright red, as I was rubbed with a towel.

Then to bed, the eldest leading with his hand around the candle to stop it blowing out, up the wooden stairs to bed.

Dad had the job of taking the bath water out in buckets to the drain outside, and hang the bath up outside. One such bath night, a banging on the door.

A man said: "I am knock-a-post. If you have the Evening Post you have won ten shilings." Showing him the paper, Mother was given the prize. It kept us in food all week.

NOTTINGHAM POOR BOYS HOME HOLIDAY BY THE SEA

Mother told my brother and me that we were going to seaside camp for a week. With our little suitcase packed, my Mother and Aunt Clara took us to Nottingham railway station.

About forty other boys got on the train. Aunt Clara gave a much older boy two shillings to look after us. We waved goodbye as the train pulled out in clouds of steam.Our first time away from home!

It was exciting watching the fields roll by. We had never been on a train before. Two burly men were in charge. They marched us from the platform at Skegness in threes like soldiers.

Near the sea and beach, there were three wooden huts with red corrugated tin roofs: one a long dormitory with lockers at each bed and sheets and blankets stacked on the bed. We were told to make our beds after a mug of tea and slice of bread. To bed at eight.

At seven next morning, our minders shouted: "Get dressed, blankets folded neatly on your bed."

After a wash, we were marched to the dining hall. Porridge, toast, marmalade and a mug of tea. Although I was very young, it sticks in my mind: the centre table had vases of flowers. And the staff were sat down. The smell of bacon! They had eggs, bacon, sausage. Special meals for them.

As we stood ready to be marched to the beach, each of us was given a grey pullover. As we marched off, I read on the pullovers NOTTINGHAM POOR BOYS HOME in red across our chests. So on the beach people took pity on us, giving our minders money to buy ice-cream.

One night it poured with rain. We could not sleep for the noise on the tin roofs. By seven at night, a mug of cocoa. In bed by eight!

It was a boring holiday but we had seen the sea. Mother met us at Nottingham. I was pleased to see her and I realised how good home was.

P.S. I think juvenile crime as it is today (1994), the young criminal when he has done wrong should be sent away from home for a few weeks. He would soon think how good life was at home.

When I was called up in the Army, the first six months away was a punishment to me and I had done no crime.

THE WEEK'S GROCERIES

On Saturday mornings, with brothers George and Tom the eldest, we took a barrow made of crate-wood built on an old pram chassis down the vale to Bulwell Market to Marsdens the grocer.

As you went in the door, there was aroma of dried fruits, home-cured bacon and the pine sawdust on the floor.

The staff dressed in white aprons and jackets. Most of them had a moustache with hair combed back. On the counter, there was a barrel shape of butter as it had come out of the cask. If you asked for a pound, a piece would be cut off and, with little wooden bats, patted into shape and wrapped in greaseproof paper.

Bacon was cut on the bright chrome slicer by turning a wheel with the right hand and catching the slices in the left one. If you asked for tea, sugar, currants or raisins, flour or rice, it was scooped out of a sack and put in a thick blue paper bag and weighed on scales. The top was folded over.

Bacon and hams hung around the walls on hooks. The grocer would tick each item off in your order book and reckon it up.

The most fascinating thing when you gave him the money was that he put it in a capsule, then placed this in a tube and pulled a chain. It shot along the tube to the cashier, then returned the same way with your change.

We would fill our barrow with a week's supply of food for a family of six for 30/- (£1.50). Next to this shop was the butcher. Outside on hooks hung pheasants, with rabbits and hares and poultry. At the rear on Pilkington Street was a slaughter house where the meat was killed.

The Market was cobble stoned. The trams came across to the shops. As we pushed our laden barrow, sheep and cattle were driven to slaughter.

If you could not fetch your groceries like we did, they would be delivered by a boy on a bike to your door. All shops delivered at no charge.

The kitchen was the most used room in the house, but no fitted carpets. Every day, the pine top table was scrubbed, as were the red quarry tiles it stood on. But in front of the coal fire was a home-made pegged rug, pushed up to the fender which stopped the hot coal dropping on to it. One Winter night, we kids were sat on the rug in front of the roaring fire.

Mother said to Dad: "We could do with making a new rug."

Dad fetched a large hessian sack. It said Tate & Lyle Sugar on it. Cutting it down the edge, he opened it up. He cleared the table, putting the paraffin lamp on the dresser. Mother helped to turn the table up-side-down, the legs up to the ceiling. He spread the sack over them, nailing the sack at each corner to the leg ends.

We kids thought it was good and crawled under it like a tent.

Mother went under the stairs and came out with a bundle of old clothes: trousers, jackets, coats etc. Dad cut them into strips about one inch wide and eight inches long. Out of the knife drawer, Dad brought out some pointed pegs. We were shown how to make two holes about one inch apart with the pointed stick and to push each end of the strip through the sack. We all sat round pegging.

Mother picked the iron poker up and knocked on the wall. At this signal Aunt Flo came in. We gave her a peg. After a while, Mother knocked on the other wall. In came Grandad.

He always had his gold watch and chain in his waistcoat pocket. With the fire, it was very hot. He pulled up a chair, took off his waistcoat and put it on the back of the chair, taking out his watch and putting it on the shelf.

We all worked very hard. It took about a week to fill all the hessian. On the Friday night, it was all set up again to finish it. Next day, Mother lay it on the yard to clip all the strip ends level.

Grandad came and said: "I am looking for my waistcoat."

"What was it like," Mother said?

"Navy pin-striped," said Grandad.

"Oh dear," said Mother looking at the flecks of pin-stripe in the rug: "Grandad it's in the rug!"

The room was special, only used when Aunts and Uncles came. But some Sundays, Dad made a fire in the room. In the centre was a polished table. Its turned legs had wool stockings on to stop anyone scratching them. A green cloth covered it, tassles hanging from the edge. The fire place was small with coloured tiles around it.

The window looked out on the garden and the railway, with trains passing day and night. Around the walls were pictures of deceased relatives, hung grimly: ladies with long hat pins stuck through their hats and lace blouses up to the chin.

Under the table was a carpet square, edged by lino to the walls. In the window was a large aspidistra plant. The room always felt cold and smelt fusty.

On the table was a well-decorated paraffin lamp. Through the glass bowl, two wicks hung. The glass funnel was covered by a round china bowl painted with flowers. With a solid brass base, it stood in the centre of the table.

Later on in life, my eldest brother was allowed in this room, on a Sunday when he brought his girl friend home. But they were not allowed to shut the door.

TRIP TO MANSFIELD HORSE FAIR

As I said earlier, the Roberts now lived in our street. George and his son George who I went to school with. Tom who had lost his wife lived with them. Early one morning, Tom knocked on our door and asked Mother if I could have the day off school as he had to go to Mansfield to see relatives.

It was a long way and he wanted company on the way. Mother gave way as it was near the school holidays. The sun was breaking through the mist as we trotted along the country lanes in the pony and trap, the white pony picking its feet up proudly.

I remember it kept lifting its tail to blow off. The smell hit our faces like manure. Through Papplewick, Linby Village on to the Mansfield Ramp-er, a main road to Mansfield. No traffic. Just the odd farm cart. People working in the fields. Tom pointed out a stone monument at the side of the road and told me the tale of a servant girl going to work on one of the large estates. She was robbed and murdered at that spot by a tramp. He was hanged for it.

We travelled a steady five miles an hour. By ten o'clock, we were near the town. As we approached an inn, Tom said he had better give the horse a rest. But I knew it was an excuse for a drink. I filled a bucket of water and gave the horse a drink and hung the nose bag on its head for it to feed. Tom brought me a bottle of pop. It had a glass marble in the top sealed tight by the gas. You pushed the marble in to break the seal.

In Mansfield it was very busy with horse drawn vehicles of every kind. I remember Tom drove behind a large hotel. At the back, it was like a cattle market: stalls, horsedrawn caravans at the end of this big field, organ music, smell of coal and smoke driving the steam engines, a fair with clouds of steam.

Tom soon found his relatives where there was a large table cloth spread on the grass, pork pies, carved ham off the bone, a joint of beef, home-baked bread and gallon jugs of beer. We were told to help ourselves.

I left them to see what was happening. Most men were in tweed jackets, bowler hats and riding breeches with a silk scarf around their neck (a muffler). Most had large moustaches.

The Shire Horses had long tails plaited with coloured ribbons, their manes as well, brasses glinting in the sun, white silk ear-muffs with long tassles swinging as they trotted. A group looking like farmers stood near the auctioneer as the horses trotted by to show off.

The auctioneer shouted: "This fine mare. Trained to plough. She's neither ring bone or spavin, side bone, a sound fit horse. What am I bid?" These things were horse diseases.

I watched the roundabouts, and a man making toffee. Then in a paddock I saw twenty wild ponies not broken in. Completely wild straight from the New Forest. And some from Wales a lad told me.

Most of these would go down the mines, probably never see the green fields again. They were tiny, just right for the low tunnels underground. As I approached, you could see fear in their eyes. They still had their long shaggy Winter coats on.

Tom bought two of the wild ponies. As we prepared to go home he tied them to the back of the trap. Shouting Goodbye to the family, we moved off, the ponies kicking and jumping as we trotted along. Then they steadied down as we drove along the lanes back to Bulwell.

It soon became dark. We stopped to light the oil lamps. It was eerie as we travelled along the dark lanes. My thoughts went back to the days of the highwayman, when he lay in wait for travellers on these roads.

Although we had our lights on, the roads were spooky. When we arrived at the stables down Church Lane, he stabled the white horse and fed him. The two wild ponies were put in the field. My Mother was pleased I was back and I told her my story.

Next day at school, Mr Sadler called me to the front of the class.

"Where were you yesterday," he asked. I told him of my day out. Giving me two sheets of paper, he said:" Go and write an essay of what you have done yesterday for the school exams."

I sat at my desk and wrote all about my day out. I gave it to him as I finished school for the day.

Mr Sadler was a stocky-built man always in a smart suit with a waistcoat with a gold chain across it. As he talked, he twisted the chain in his fingers. He was a very strict teacher. As he entered next day, we all stood up. He called the register. We sat down.

"Cross," he shouted: "Come to my desk."

With a lump in my throat, I stood there. He lifted the lid of his desk. I thought he was getting out the strap. He passed me my essay.

He said: "Read it to the class."

In a trembly voice, I read it very slowly. Then there was silence. Standing up, he took the papers off me, and wrote on them before passing them back to me: "Very good work 19 out of 20."

There were giggles in the classroom.

He turned and said: "A very interesting story." Mother was pleased.

"It was not a day wasted, then" she said.

After school, young George and I went to the stables. Tom and George had the wild ponies on long reins, training and controlling them. The slow task of putting a saddle on their backs and then riding them like you see cowboys with bucking broncos. After a few weeks we could ride them down the lanes.

At weekends, we travelled the countryside, selling barrels for ponch tubs, and steel drums for water butts. Buying and selling was their trade. They bought damaged barrels from factories, repaired some and cut the tops off others to make feeding troughs. The bottom halves made wash tubs.

They bought dogs and broken carts. We repaired, painted and varnished and sold again. At a house in Chatham Street they bought an ice-cream churn, and made and sold it off a barrow. There was no hygiene, no fridges, yet you never heard of food poisoning. No antibiotics, just old fashioned remedies.

WE WALKED EVERYWHERE

Bulwell was surrounded by farms.

A favourite Sunday walk was towards Cinderhill pit and brickworks. Opposite Bagnall Lane, a farm track took you in a circle through Hootons Farm to come out at Bulwell Cemetery and a deep quarry for clay to make bricks at Babbington Brick Company.

On this walk we were near corn, potatoes and turnips. We called turnips donies. Pull one up, peel it and and eat it like an apple. Around one corner, there was a small valley with spring streams. On a hot day, we would take our shoes off and paddle. And there was an old derelict barn which we thought was haunted. We ran by it.

An interesting hobby was collecting birds eggs. It was not illegal then. With a needle, you made a small hole at each end of an egg, blow the yoke out and the egg was ready for storing. We kept this delicate collection in sawdust in a cardboard box.

We had learnt the mistake of putting eggs in our pockets. They broke. We put them in our caps in a row in the peak of the cap. One day our walk had been very succesful. A yellow hammer's, linnet's, bullfinch's and two plovers' eggs.

The farmer said: "I hope you haven't been in my fields flattening the corn."

"No sir," we said.

"Good lads," he said as he passed us tapping our caps with his stick and walked away smiling. We had egg yoke running down our face all the way home.

The plover was a large black and white bird. It laid three eggs in the furrows in a ploughed field. We watched them land and then ran to the nest. They were big eggs. You could eat them. They were rich and tasty.

Later on when I was in my teens, we did the same walk on a Sunday but with girl friends. We didn't do a lot of birdnesting then!

THE MIRACLE OF LIGHT

One day gas was laid along the terrace. Then we had two gas lamps over the fire place and one in the centre of the ceiling.

The house was now very bright at night. It took a lot of getting used to

Another good thing was a sink was put in the corner near the window with a cold water tap. It was marvellous. No more carrying water out or in the bucket. Also we now had a wind-up gramophone, with a large green horn to amplify the sound.

The gas lights had delicate gas mantles. They dropped to bits if you touched them with a match when lighting them. But it was pleasant to read at night.

With Dad and my brother George and Tom now working, Mother bought a brand new piano. It was put in the front room. It cost 49 guineas. She paid a man in installments every Friday. Tom was already playing the violin. So George was to have lessons on the new piano. After a year, they could accompany each other for Sunday nights' entertainment.

Things were looking up after the struggle.

Now a new washing mashine came on the scene. It was a galvanised tub on four legs. The small mangle had rubber rollers. Lift up the lid, and there were four steel paddles. Put in boiling water with soap, close the lid and turn the paddles with a handle on top, back and forth, about forty times. Pull the clothes out of the tub and push through them through the mangle. The water from them ran back into the tub. Rinsing was done in the same way. It was an improvement but still hard work.

Wonders never cease!

The gas was taken out and the house wired for electric lights. We thought it was wonderful. The gramophone went and in came the wireless receiver. I shall never forget the name of it: Umello. You turned it round on a spinner to get the station. It had wet batteries in the back, charged by a trickle charger.

I remember Dad saying: "Turn that thing down, it's going too fast."

Now the family was growing up. Mother was interested in getting a better house. I was thirteen. I had an errand boy's job at the local butchers.

PART 2

PAID WORK BEGINS

THE BUTCHER'S BOY

One of my jobs was cutting meat off bones till they were clean.

Meat was put on display in the window. But stored over night, it went dark. So each joint had a thin slice cut off to make it look fresh. The slice was put with the meat off the bones into the mincer for sausage meat.

I had a butcher's white coat with striped apron. I think Mother would have liked me to go into business in shops.

The butcher's bike was big and heavy, with a carrier back and front and a nameplate. It was too big for me to ride at first. But after falling off twice, I mastered it. I went all day Saturday and every night after school for five shillings a week.

One day I was delivering meat. As I came round a corner, a girl shouted to me. I looked back to shout at her. When I turned back, I was going down a steep hill. I hit a man wheeling a barrow of muck with my front wheel. He fell in the barrow and rolled down the hill.

I could hear the girl laughing.

BIKING

At thirteen, it was a year until leaving school. Twelve of us, six boys and six girls, would meet at nights and weekends. But they all had bikes, which was the main means of transport.

Now I was earning a few shillings at the butchers, I went to the bike shop on Highbury Vale. Mr.Robinson let me have a second-hand bike for ten shillings for a shilling a week. He gave me a card to mark off each week.

I was proud of the bike, a Rudge Whitworth: chrome handle bars, a leather seat. I painted and polished it till it looked like new. On Sunday, with the gang, we would take the road to Matlock.

Most of us wore shorts for cylcing. The girls wore shorts with ankle socks, silk blouses and a band around the hair. No traffic worries - nothing on the road on hot Summer days except horses and carts.

Our gang all lived on Highbury Vale. We had been brought up together.

The Depression had lifted. Raleigh Cycles was having a boom. Exports were good. Everyone wanted a bike.

With talking pictures, all the film stars smoked. Teenagers copied. Players cigarettes were being exported too. Factories were busy making silk stockings and cloth for new fashion clothes. Things were great. Some cycle clubs had as many as forty members on the road.

1932. One day, as I sat at my school desk, the headmaster sent for me. A man and woman sat in his office. They were introduced as Mr and Mrs Clayton. They had a shop on Picadilly on Highbury Vale. They wanted a lad to learn the trade.

I was let off school to start work. I was pleased to get a job so quickly. I started work on Monday morning at 6.0 a.m. putting milk into bottles, then delivering it. At 10.0, a bread round. At 2.0 the groceries went out. Then 6.0 o'clock the later milk round: seven days a week for 15/-.

They wanted a slave not someone to learn the trade. I had been conned.

So I went with my mates to Raleigh Cycles. And we were out every night for walks, talking pictures or cycling. We were now young men, so we went for a hot slipper bath every Saturday (1/- including soap and towel) at the Northern Baths which were quite near.

Mother had her wish. We moved up the street to a larger house, but still no bath or inside toilet, but we had more room. All the rooms were large and there was a long garden. All the family were now working and Mother was happy with the money coming in and the new house.

I will never forget the Sundays all the family sat down for tea in the large front room. There was a white cloth trimmed with lace on the long table in the centre, a cake stand full of fancy cakes, cut glass bowls of salmon, peaches, trifle and always a bowl of custard, ham on the bone with Dad carving, plates of white and brown bread cut corner to corner... The best china tea service set out on the table.

And above all a tall vase of celery, like a bowl of flowers. The centre of the celery was tender, not like the tough stringy outside sticks.

Mother would say: "Don't eat all the heart. Take some of the outside sticks."

The strict rule: nobody left the table until everyone was finished. They were happy days. Tom was courting with plans on marriage.

FIRST DATE

I worked at Raleigh, on a mass production method. Boring job! Putting parts on three speed gears. But it was eight to five, not like the shop job never done.

At work, a new girl was working opposite me on the conveyor. I had to help her and show her what to do. She was very good looking and blonde.

I always seemed to make friends with blondes. It was Summer time. I asked her what she did at night. She said she had a new bike.

I plucked up courage and asked would she go for a ride with me. So we made my first real date for seven o'clock the next night, to meet at Cinderhill crossroads. Looking back, she cycled a long way: from Dunkirk near Beeston along the Western Boulevard to Cinderhill.

I was in the kitchen cleaning my teeth. Brylcream on my hair.

Mother said to Dad: "He's got a date."

I blushed and was out on my bike quickly to meet my date. I can still see her in my memory standing with her bike at the crossroads, her blonde hair held back by a ribbon across her forehead.

We walked with our bikes along country lanes. She had make-up on like all the girls copying the stars on the cinema, with eye brows plucked and false ones painted on, lipstick, rouge and the strong smell of Evening in Paris perfume.

At first we were both shy. We dropped our bikes on the grass near a small stream near the cover of a hawthorn bush. The sun was still hot. We talked about work. As I lay back, she tormented me with a long grass stalk, tickling me. As I leaned over to take it off her, we lay in a lingering kiss.

At nine o'clock we wandered back to the crossroads and a farewell kiss. She had to be in by ten o'clock and had a long way to ride.

That night, I couldn't sleep. I was in love! I was sixteen now.

On Saturday nights, we met in the city outside the new Ritz cinema. She looked beautiful in a dress. It was around two shillings each to go in. We walked down to the plush seats holding hands.

At the interval, the electric organ rose up in front of the screen. Jack Helyer would play while we had chocolates and ice-cream. I would see her to the bus. On Sundays we would walk in Wollaton Park.

Life was getting better each year with us all working, good food, good clothes, new bikes. We soon forgot the poverty we had as children. Alma was moved to another department: our puppy love faded as quickly as it had started.

Some people could afford a new car. The price then: around £100.

NEW JOB: WORKING IN WOOD

I left Raleigh to work at a small builders in Lincoln Street, Basford. I was sent a message from Raleigh a year later to say Alma had got married. The new job was very interesting as I liked working in wood. We made Sycamore wood leg boards, for hosiery firms and large oak vats for bleaching and dyeing machines.

The first choice of working in Nottingham was Players cigarettes, Boots the Chemist and Raleigh, but they had a reputation of setting on school leavers then sacking them when the next batch left school. Co-op was a good job too. But I liked my job at Hopewells Builders.

When silk sockings were made, the shape had to be formed in steam presses. Stockings were pulled on thin boards shaped as a woman's leg. We made these thin Sycamore wood shapes.

At the yard, my job was to start at 6.0 a.m. to get steam up in the boiler by lighting the fires in the two tubes in the Lancaster boiler. I piled shavings and coal on till I saw the dial finger on 95lb pressure.

The workmen started work at 8.0 a.m. I pulled a chain for the steam hooter for the start (and finish) of work. I would go into the engine room. I would turn a valve in a cloud of steam. The long piston would turn the giant wheel until it was at a speed controlled by governors. A belt from this wheel would turn the underground shafts to work the machines. This steam engine is now in Wollaton Museum.

The Sycamore leg boards were sanded down on sanding discs, covering you with a fine white dust.

Sometimes I was that interested in my job, I would forget to stoke the boiler. The circular saw would come slowly to a halt for lack of steam.

The firm was also undertakers, making coffins. You soon learned to keep an eye on the office. If we saw a person come to the office with a handkerchief to their eyes, we would go and hide in the woodshed because the undertaker always took a boy to measure the body.

Then you had to work with the undertaker as his mate to make the coffin and put the body in. When the coffin was nearly made, he would send you to the blacksmith with a cauldron of tar to melt it on the fire. Then it had to be carried back, up steps, the smell filling the room. Pouring the hot tar into the bare coffin, Percy the undertaker would spread it into the corners to seal the wood joints. He always left a lump of wood at the head of the coffin. One day I asked him why he did this.

He said: "My lad, when the eternal trumpets blow, when the dead rise up to walk, all those I've buried will have a better start with their heads raised higher."

One morning, a woman came out of the office wiping tears from her eyes. I felt a tap on my shoulder. It was Percy Brown.

"I can't find a lad anywhere," he said. "Get your coat, come with me. I was stoking the boiler and put my shovel down and followed him. "Bring those folding trestles and a six-foot board," he said.

I struggled walking behind. We only went to the next street. Percy knocked on the door. An old man said:" she's in the front room."

As my eyes adjusted to the light, I could see a bed with a bedspread pulled up to the headboard. He told me to open the trestles and put the board on them by the side on the bed.

He suddenly pulled the bedspread back. I was shocked. There lay a frail old lady in a nightdress. She was so thin, I had not seen her under the clothes. He measured her chest and length with a tape measure. He put a strap over his head, threading it under her shoulders.

"Get hold of her feet, lad," he said sternly. "When I say lift, lift."

As he lifted his head, the strap lifted her body, swinging her on to the trestle. As she lay, there was a long moaning sigh and a terrible stench. I was out of the door like a shot. Percy explained to me that, with moving the body, her bloated stomach had blown gas out of her mouth. That was the moaning sound.

I could see the reason for hiding in the woodshed!

When the coffin was made with my help, we took it to the house, and put the body in. The shroud was split so you could put it over the arms and tuck it in the silk padding. A veil was placed over the face. The lid was left off for relatives to view. Then on the day of the funeral, Percy, in his black suit and top hat, would screw it down.

A long while after, I learnt that Percy had no sense of smell due to an accident on a motor bike as a lad. No wonder the smell never bothered him! This experience taught me to be more alert watching the office!

I was now interested in making small coffee tables etc and it grieved me to see the lovely oak and elm wood to be buried. I used to think what I could make with it.

One day Percy told me to deliver a parcel to the Workhouse on Highbury Vale (now the Hospital). It was covered in brown paper. When I arrived at the gate, I was told to take it to the mortuary. To my surprise, when uncovered, I saw it was a small coffin for a baby. This one had been stillborn. I was told they put them in a grave when a funeral was in progress.

For many funerals, four black horses pulled the hearse, black muffs with tassles on their ears; followed by hansom cabs pulled by black horses. The hearse had glass sides with small brass pillows to stop the coffin sliding. The funeral bearers and undertaker wore long black coats and top hats. Neighbours would stand at their doors in shawls and flat caps. There was always a street collection for a wreath. They watched as the coffin was brought out of the front room.

The wheelwright made cart wheels for all the carts on the road. The wheel had to have steel hoops on for the road. It was a tricky job getting them on. Saturdays were picked for this operation. Waste wood was put in a narrow furnace and the steel hoops rolled in. They got white hot. The newly made wheel was laid on a steel platform and screwed tight.

The blacksmith would say: "Ready, lads." With long tongs, he would pull the hoop out of the fire and roll it on to the wheel and quickly hammer it down over the new wheel which caught fire.

Then he would yell: "Water, Water!"

Us lads would keep dowsing the hot steel to cool it. You could hear the spokes tighten and creak as the steel hoop contracted as it went cold. It was a very precise job. If the blacksmith had been a bit out with the measurement it would have been too small or too large. These were tradesmen.

GLADYS

I was now nearly seventeen. The new job was very interesting as I liked working in wood. I spent a lot of time in Basford, working and courting there with Gladys who lived in Vernon Avenue.

My mate and I started going out with Marie Wardle from Hucknall and Gladys Buxton from Basford. As usual, I picked the blonde, Gladys. She was a real smasher.

My Dad's family all came from Basford. I went in the Pear Tree Pub on Bulwell Lane. This was their local, although I didn't know them.

In my out-of-work time, I was back with the old gang I was at school with. We still did cycle clubbing. There was not yet a lot of traffic on the roads.

Carnival bands were the scene now with their colourful uniforms and drum major. We were like football fans, following them.

At the cinema were gangster films. James Cagney, George Raft and Humphry Bogart were our pin-ups so the fashion was to dress like them in "Black Ace" top coats which came down to our shoes and with heavy padded shoulders and slim waist.

With a white silk scarf and a trilby hat (with a little feather) pulled down over one eye, we looked like gangsters.

The girls copied the female stars with heavy make-up, permanent waves, plucked eye brows and silk stockings with suspenders, and always a cigarette in the mouth.

CALLED UP

Before the main film at the Cinema, there was Movietone News from around the world. At eighteen, it was hard to believe Hitler taking the salute to his massive array of soldiers. Thousands of tanks and guns parading the streets with his large airforce and navy with submarines - a threat to the world. But no one took any notice, not even America. The Government said there won't be another war. We were even exporting scrap iron to Germany to help build this danger.

When the Government woke up to the dangers of possible air raids, sectional iron air raid shelters were available for families to bury in their back garden. As Hitler threatened small countries around his borders, the world did not seem to bother.

Tom, George and I dug a hole and helped Dad erect the air raid shelter and cover it with soil. I thought at the time that they could soon fill with water. They must have been damp and dismal places in an air raid with just candles for light and warmth. Would history repeat itself? To most people, the last terrible war was still in their minds.

Then in June 1939 came a letter commanding me to go for a medical examination in Nottingham.

At the beginning of July came a letter with a railway warrant. I was to report to Hereford for training. On July 16th I left to be trained on the aircraft defence of Britain.

It took the British Government two or three years to realise what the man in the street knew would happen. Hitler had a marvellous new toy that the world had let him produce. Now he was going to play with it. The special trains left Nottingham packed with young men aged twenty to do six months training and then go into the Reserve. They still thought there would be no war.

At Hereford Station, Army sergeants marched us on to buses. We pulled up on the Racecourse. It was covered with white bell tents not even camouflaged tents.

We were given 1914 uniforms left over from that terrible war. All the fighting equipment was out-of-date. The Army had not modernised one bit. Food was rationed. Our eating utensils a tin bowl and two tin plates (the same as prisoners had in jail). Some lorries were so old they had solid rubber tyres and some gun carriages had cart wheels designed to be drawn by horses. So this was the British Army: the job I said I would never do after seeing how the old soldiers of the 1914-18 war suffered in my childhood.

I was taken from home, a young man now, just as things were getting better. I had a girl friend but things were so uncertain now, I wrote to finish our friendship.

In my opinion, those in Government in pre-war years should have been tried for treason for failing to defend Britain. Here we stood on the brink of war dressed in riding breeches, puttees wrapped from knees to boots, and old tunics with brass buttons meant for horse artillery. And we hadn't got a horse.

We looked like ghosts of the men who had fought in the First World War. History was to repeat itself.

PART 3

WARTIME

After the surprise and the disgust, poor food, small rations, the wrong and constantly wet clothes, nine men trying to sleep in a bell tent through pouring rain through July and August, ankle deep in mud: we were made into soldiers by instructors who begrudged leaving their regular units. These sergeants and corporals were drawn from every regiment of the Army.

Sunday, September 3rd 1939 there was a church parade with the band playing followed by about three hundred young soldiers. We marched through the City of Hereford to the Cathedral.

The service was stopped in the middle of hymn singing. The Colonel said we were now at war with Germany. Everyone cheered.

Back at camp, panic stations as if the Germans were coming. We were issued with five rounds and taken by lorry with our rifles to railway bridges and important buildings to spend a miserable night on guard.

The British Expeditionary Force was sent to France. Territorials and Militia men with obsolete 1914 equipment and methods against a highly trained mechanised force with an Air Force trained to co-operate with tanks and guns. The British dug in like the previous war. Nothing happened for months. Then this powerful German force blasted through towns and villages like a tornado, through Holland, Belgium and France taking thousands of poorly equipped soldiers and pinning the BEF to the coast at Dunkirk.

We had seven days leave. I remember coming home in my riding breeches and tunic. Someone said: "Where's you left your horse?" The pubs were full. The war scare was on. Some people,

including friends and family, said: "It will be over in a few months."
I never thought it would take so long as it did.

Back at camp, we packed our kit and were marched to a train. Not knowing where we were going as the stations rolled by with no station names displayed. At one station, we were told to disembark. We found out we were at Louth near the East coast. At the side of the station was a camp Headquaters of the 44th Leicestershire Regiment.

After a couple of days, eight of us were told to put our bedding and kit in a lorry, and we scrambled in at the side of a searchlight. Towed at the back was a large diesel generator to make power for the powerful light. There was just a Lance Corporal in charge. The weather was getting bitterly cold.

At three in the afternoon, we pulled on to a field off a country lane. It was a desolate site except for one large farm house in the distance.

In the long bare wooden hut, we dropped our blankets and kit to mark our claim of where to sleep on the floor. In the centre was a tall iron combustion stove. We found out later this was to be our central heating, water boiler, toaster - to be fed night and day by hedgerow timber. No coal was provided. Outside it was bitterly cold and snow was falling.

The equipment was spaced out in the field. At one end, the sound locator: three wooden trumpets to pick up the sound of planes. At each side was a swivel chair for the spotter with binoculars to find the plane and guide the searchlight beam on to it. There was a soldier to push the switch to expose the beam and watch the carbons burn to throw the light off the large mirror into the sky. A long arm with a steering wheel moved the searchlight on to the target. A thick rubber cable from the light trailed three hundred

The searchlight crew.
Bill third from left

yards down the lane to the power generator. For an electrical reason, it had to be that distance.

We were now ready for action. One man was put on guard with rifle and five rounds. We laid our blankets out, the stove was getting warm, so a dixie of water was put on to boil. We had six white petrol cans marked WATER. And a green box with our rations of food. It took the dixie two hours to boil. Someone made some cheese sandwiches, and in the box was tomorrow's breakfast and dinner.

The Lance Corporal, 'one stripe', in charge was older than us, about twenty-six. Like us, he had no idea. We had been dumped

74

in this field, no contact with Headquaters, no telephone. It was like being marooned on a desert island.

The door opened. A blast of cold air. The shout of "Action." A plane! Everyone ran to their posts. The generator man had to run three hundred yards to get the power for the light. An exposed beam shot into the sky. The plane signalled a morse letter of the day and recognition lights: it was one of ours, friendly.

Bill on guard.

We lay on our blankets, cold and wet, gas mask on our chest, wearing greatcoats and wellingtons, hungry and tired. The next man went on guard for two hours. We turned out three times for false alarms.

As dawn broke, snow was falling. The Corporal said:" I want a volunteer to cook breakfast and get dinner ready." Nobody answered,

75

so he detailed one, and said everyone must take a turn in the cookhouse which had no stove but all the utensils, table, knives, frying pans, baking tins.

A shallow hole was dug in the ground and filled with twigs and branches. Diesel oil was poured on to the damp wood to get it to burn. We found an iron grating to put over the fire to stand the dixies on. Dinner was stew. It tasted of diesel oil. Followed by rice pudding. The rice had not been soaked. It was hard and gritty.

We had two cans of water left. They were emptied into a galvansied bowl and put on the stove to hot up. We all had to wash and shave in the same water.

Standing in the field in the biting wind, the two-hour guard was boring. We had an obsolete Lewis Machine Gun in training. It misfired more often than it fired but it was all we had against low flying aircraft. To keep warm, we built a sandbag wall around it in case we were attacked.

A lorry pulled on to the site.

Dropping the tailboard, the driver said: "Come and fetch these."

A green ration tin and eight cans of water, diesel oil, paraffin for the hurrican lamps, some letters for us. He took the empty cans and ration tin to fill up at Headquarters. He said he would come every day. If we had letters to post or clothing to exchange, he'd take it in.

We asked him if there was a shop near. There was a small village about a mile down the road. The Corporal sent one man to the shops as we were out of fags, razor blades, writing paper and envelopes, soap and toothpaste. It took him about two hours there and back.

Was this England? Dumped in a field, no contact with the outside world. Just like cattle in a field, fed and watered each day. We had power to produce enough electricity to light up a small town and we had to try to read by hurrican lamps. With just a bit of thought, we could have had electirc light and electric stove for lighting and heating. But we were still in the First World War time zone. Everything was out of date.

The weather became worse. Snow drifted across the huts. Fuel was getting harder to find. But we found a bowsaw, so we could now cut some trees. Each man on guard was told to cut twenty logs. The bowl on the stove was filled up with snow. Now we had penty of water. The snow paddled in. The hut floor was awash making our blankets wet. Some of the drifting snow was ten foot high. We dug a channel to the gun pit and equipment. We were snow bound.

We realised nobody could reach us. Food and diesel was running out. Then we saw a figure stagger through the field. It was the ration driver. He was stuck in a drift near the village. Six of us took a duck board to use as a sledge. We pulled the rations and fuel slowly back each day for about a week. It was like being in Siberia.

An Officer, (one-pip) Lieutenant, visited us twice. He said: "Good show chaps. You are doing a good job." Then in his car back to the warmth of Headquaters!

We had been there about a month, the food the same each day: stew then prunes and rice. After each one of us had a day as cook, it was decided I gave them the best meal. Thanks to my childhood and my Mother who taught me, I was elected cook. For a change one day, I threw a dozen large potatoes in the wood

Desolate site. Bill fourth from left.

embers of the fire. When cooked, they were cut open with margarine and a thick slice of cheese. They all came back for more.

The toilet, a trench two feet deep had been dug when we arrived with a piece of hessian sack around two posts and a pole across two oil drums. It was getting full. We could only cover it with snow. The ground was too hard to dig a new trench.

We were beginning to smell through lack of a bath. The snow helped the water shortage but it also carried into the hut, making it cold and wet. On top of this, lack of sleep. Apart from the two hour guard, every plane which came over at night had to be challenged with the beam. The only time we took our clothes off was when the laundry came each week.

Snowbound. Bill fourth from left.

As I patrolled on guard, I saw blood on the white snow. I followed the trail to find a dead rabbit. It had blood on its jaws from trying to eat thorns from the top of the hedges sticking out from the snow.

If we had been in the frontline in France, this situation would have been understandable. But this was England. What good were we doing? We never saw any night fighters. If we exposed our beam on an enemy plane, what would have happened? There were no anti-aircraft guns.

The despatch rider who came every day to tell us the aircraft recognition signals told us some of the roads had been cleared by snow plough but he had parked his bike at a large house on the hill and walked about a mile to us. Our Corporal was a very quiet man. He read out a letter from the lady of that house inviting two of us to lunch on Boxing Day. Then we realised it was Christmas Day and we had stew again!

On Boxing Day, myself and Wilday were off duty. We had a good wash and put on our best uniform - riding breeches etc! We had to be there by twelve o'clock. In our Wellington Boots, we struggled to the road, first time out for a month. After about an hour, we came to the drive way of the house: two small soldiers standing in the doorway of this Victorian house.

As we stood in the doorway, visions of turkey and Christmas pudding! The door opened. The butler looked at us. "Come this way," he said. He led us along the hallway with large paintings on the walls into a room of antique furnishings, large palm plants and a roaring log fire.

He pointed to our Wellingtons. We took them off and he walked away with them, coming back with a tray with two glasses of sherry. After being in the cold, our faces were aglow.

Then the door opened slowly again. It was the butler with a wheelchair. In it, a young man with a twisted body and a large head, followed by a grey-haired old lady with strings of pearls at her neck. She introduced herself and shook our hands.

Going to the wheechair, she said: "This is my son, he can't speak." We tried not to look at him.

She said: "I can just see your camp from the bedroom window. It looks so desolate."

The door opened again. The maid said: "Dinner is served." The old lady told the butler to get us another drink. She went out of the room and the butler beckoned us to follow.

We sat at the dining table, two crystal chandeliers above our heads. The lady said her son had been like that from birth, but she had two other sons serving as very senior officers in the Army.

80

Wilday and I sat opposite each other, the lady at the head of the table. The young maid came in and filled our glasses with wine. The food was served from a long sideboard. First soup (we now had visions of the turkey).

The butler came in with a meat tray covered with a silver dome to keep the meat hot. As he lifted it off, a small piece of brisket which he began to carve putting two pieces on each plate. The maid filled it up with vegetables and served it. They went out of the room. When we had cleared our plates, they entered with steam pudding and the butler filled our glasses up.

The lady stood up and gave us a small cigar and then left us.

Wilday whispered: "Where's the bloody turkey then?"

We saw a button on the table leg. We pushed it. It was the bell to the kitchen.

In came the maid: "Did you ring, Sir?"

She gave a little giggle. The butler helped us put on our greatcoats. Our Wellingtons were near the door. The lady came to say goodbye and gave us a parcel each. As we marched back, at least we had seen some civilisation! In the parcel was two pairs of socks and a balaclava head warmer.

The lads said: "Have you brought any turkey legs back?"

We realised later, the gentry have lunch and the main meal is at night. That was when the turkey would be served.

After a few more months at this site, we were told to start packing and be prepared to move.

INVASION SCARE: 1940

After enduring that terrible winter, in June 1940 for some unknown reason the site was abandoned and we came into Headquaters in Spalding. It was heaven. Hot showers, good food eaten in a dining room, beds to sleep in and, best of all, to go into Spalding town and have a few pints. I was only seven stone in weight at the time. We would be here until August on anti-parachute patrols.

Three of us were sitting on our beds surrounded by our kits.

In came the Sergeant Major and said: "You have been brought into Headquaters to do a special operation. The Colonel is forming an anti-parachute defence. We have intelligence reports of German paratroops preparing to land in England, and hundreds of assault craft forming up on the French coast. Troops could be dropped at any time by planes from French airfields."

He told us the situation was so serious because troops in Britain had very little equipment to oppose the enemy. At Dunkirk, thousands of allied troops were rescued. But they had to leave their guns, rifles amd tanks in France: in fact all their equipment.

So, from all the searchlight sites, all rifles and ammo was being called in to send to the Infantry, leaving them with just a Lewis Machine Gun.

"You three are going to be the enemy," he said. "I shall take you out each day in the van, then phone a map reference to Headquarters. The Anti Para Squad will come to capture you."

He said that three civilian lorries had been comandeered, their windscreens removed so as to fire through. These would transport about thirty soldiers, the Anti Para Squad, to any area the enemy drops to invade.

"For training, we shall be the decoy German troops. As we are going to work together, there will be no formalities." He passed round his cigarettes, and said he was Fred. We three muskateers were Joe, Frank and me.

The training started after a weekend, so we went into Spalding for a boozy weekend. Monday morning, we picked up haversack rations to eat on our first excercise as decoy enemy paratroops. Fred brought the utility van and we took off. Travelling along the narrow Fenland roads, with draining ditches either side, groups of men were erecting poles in the flat fields. Fred said they were not for telephones but to stop enemy aircraft landing, because these were ideal landing grounds for gliders or troop carrying planes.

At a crossroads there were concrete pillboxes with slits for firing out across the fields. Large concrete blocks were placed on the road to make enemy tanks slow down to zig-zag between them. At a searchlight site, we noticed an old farm cart, a pole lying across it pointing to the sky.

"That's a good idea," said Fred. "From the sky it will look like an anti-aircraft gun."

We came to a sleepy village midday. Nobody about.

Let's find out where we are," said Fred spreading the map across the bonnet of the van. "This is it. This is the map ref. number we will phone to HQ," he said and wrote it down.

Hiding the van in a small wood and covered in bracken, we strolled down the village street. Joe said he was starving. Still nobody about.

"Difficult to think there is a war on," said Frank.

Our attention was drawn to a creaking sign above us "The Royal Oak. Bullards Fine Ales."

I said to Fred: "Don't you think we should go in here to see if there is a phone." Sergeant Major leading, we couldn't get in fast enough! It was dark after coming in from the bright sunshine. As our eyes became accustomed, we saw the low beamed room with old arm chairs and pictures on the wall.

A red-faced farmer type chap came in from the kitchen, a large beer belly in front of him. "What will it be soldiers?"

Fred ordered four pints. The man returned with a bucket of ale, dipping the pint pots in the beer and then banged them on the table. "That will be three shillings and four pence."

We opened the haversack rations, corned beef as usual.

Fred said: "Things must be very serious. The C.O's had a secret dispatch. All road signs are to be removed so as to delay the enemy. All vehicles left unattended must have their rotar arms removed because the paratroops will be looking for transport. Beware the enemy could be dressed as a civiliam, a policeman or even a nun!"

I said: "It is 2.30 and we better get a move on."

Fred said: "Just a minute, it's your pay. Get them in while I phone the reference number on the map to HQ. It will make it easy for them to find us."

We came out into the brilliant sun, shading our eyes. We went to the van. Fred said they would leave it there but take the rotar arm out and then they would spread separately across the fields.With the heat and the beer, we didn't get far. Within an hour we were all back in the village captured.

The Colonel praised the Sergeant Major: "Good show, chaps."

The training went on for a month and then the decoy team, to their dismay, were stood down. The Anti Para Squad were ready if the enemy landed.

Now there were lectures by an Intelligence Officer. Two soldiers from each searchlight team came into HQ. In the lecture room on the wall were large posters depicting enemy paratroopers. Across their chests were sticks of grenades, a sub-machine gun and belts of ammo. In large letters it said KNOW YOUR ENEMY.

The Officer said he had been in occupied countries with resistance fighters. From a bundle of pipes, he held one up. It had an old type long bayonet welded on.

He said: "This is to replace the rifle you sent into HQ. This is called the pike. You use it like you were taught with a rifle. When the para first lands, you can take him by surprise when he is most vulnerable. Come from the hedgerows with your pike to get his gun."

A voice chirped up: "I bet he would be surprised to see our secret weapon." There were giggles in the classroom. These pikes were sent out to all sites to defend Britain against the threat of invasion.

The Instructor went on: "To disable a tank, look around for a long piece of metal, a girder. Two of you stand in an entry. As the tank passes, thrust the metal into the tank tracks. It will fetch the treads off. It can't carry on. But, better still, if you can mount the tank, bang on the lid. When they open it, drop a petrol bomb in. If a petrol bomb is thrown in the tracks, it will burn the rubber rollers to disable it."

"We are being trained as a suicide squad," said I.

Next day more men came in for lectures. Outside there was a demonstration of how to make Molotov Cocktails. A crate of empty wine and spirit bottles were filled with petrol. We were shown how to put a rag fuse in. A large match like the bonfire match we had as kids was taped to the bottle ready for ignition.

These lectures went on until all the soldiers had some idea of how to outwit the enemy because he was expected to land, to surprise us. But, now, hadn't we got a big surprise for him!

The final excercise for the invasion threat was the Colonel's brainchild. If we were overun by the enemy, we were to fight on, under cover, at night. We were to carry out sabotage. We would have to build a secret hideout. He selected a spot in a small wooded area.

We set to work digging a large hole about the size of your living room, then covered it with corrugated sheets, soil and bracken. With a secret entrance, inside was stored water, tinned food, grenades, petrol bombs, pikes etc. Now we were prepared for the worst to happen.

Then a bolt from the blue, Hitler declared war on Russia.

Joe and Frank were posted away. I stayed at Spalding. But a new threat came to Britain. Hitler turned his powerful airforce on to London.

I was posted from Headquarters to a new site in Lincolnshire.

I had just been relieved off guard duty. It was 6.O a.m., the crew were all asleep after being called out several times during the night. Every plane that came over had to be challenged by the powerful beam. They had all been friendly. After showing their recognition lights, the beam was dowsed.

In a shed called the cookhouse, I lit a fire in the iron stove piling on sticks collected from the hedgerows. Filling a dixie from a can marked WATER, I put it on to boil. I was elected camp cook among other duties and breakfast was to be bacon, fried bread and porridge.

Pouring boiling water on the tea in the bucket, with a dash of Carnation milk, I carried it to the large wooden hut where the men lay sleeping. As I opened the door, a blast of foul air: cigarette smoke, bowel gas, sweaty feet. I took down the blackout shutters. There were moans and groans. About eight bodies lay in a row still in their greatcoats, gas masks on their chests because they could never go to bed. At the sound of a plane's engine, a whistle blew and they had to be out to challenge it with the beam.

After breakfast, the corporal laid out the duty of each man. One to relieve the guard, one to go to post letters and bring essentials, one to collect wood for the cookhouse, another to dig a fresh trench for the toilet, the rest to maintain the searchlight and locator, and clean the Lewis Machine Gun which was kept ready for firing in case of low flying aricraft.

About eleven o'clcok, a lorry pulled on site. It was Bert the ration truck driver, a real cockney lad with his gossip. I opened the ration box: potatoes, dried peas, tea, sugar, Carnation milk, carrots, a lump of meat for stew, even toilet paper... By dinner time, the day was getting very warm. They all gathered near the cookhouse for a mug of tea.

The Corporal, reading the morning paper, said: "Thay have started bombing London. Some planes have got through to the centre."

By now, the sound locator with its large bell-shaped ears to pick up engine noise of planes had been modified. The newly invented RADAR - this secret invention - not only picked up sound but the image. By transmitting radio waves into the sky, any metal object was picked up on a small screen as a bleep. By the bleep, it was possible to tell whether it was friend or foe. The sound locator and the searchlight, like robots, followed the RADAR in remote control.

On guard in the machine gun pit leaning against the sandbags with powerful binoculars, I saw a motor bike at a distance coming down the lane following a General Motors Company lorry. This was a large American built lorry.

As they pulled into the gateway of the field, an Officer jumped down. He had a large clip board. Through the binoculars, he watched his mates loading the lorry with bedding and kits. We were moving! The searchlight was pulled up the ramps on to the lorry, the generator towed behind. I loaded my blankets and kitbag. Another lorry came through the gate. The sound locator with its secrets was clipped on behind. The site was now stripped bare.

The Officer shouted: "Embark." I thought: "Where are we going now?" The soldier is always kept in suspense. What was going on? Two lorries ready to move off. Ten puzzled men lying on the grass. An Officer studying maps. It was nine o'clock and getting dusk as we moved off.

There were no road signs to give us a clue. With the invasion scare, they had been removed. As the early morning light came through, we were travelling through a large town with traffic and buses, people on the pavements going to work, some waving.

One bright spark said: "I know where we are going. To London." He was right.

As the convoy pulled into a large park, there were tennis courts and pavilions. At the far end, a row of barrack huts. And near to a large Nissen hut marked Ammunition Dump were four anti-aircraft guns with the locator and searchlight fixed at the side of them.

A Sergeant Dilks was to take charge of us. He allocated Hut No 7 to put our kit in. No beds. We were to sleep on the floor. It had been a sports store room. There was a locker marked Cricket Bats and another Footballs.

We were sent over to the pavilion with our mess tins for a meal. We hadn't eaten since the start of the journey. As we lay on the grass in the brilliant sunshine, there was the wailing of sirens. This was the first time we had heard it. An air raid!

The drone of planes overhead. They were only a few hundred feet above us in a complete "V" formation. We were dumbfounded and could not believe it was the enemy. But we could see the German crosses clearly.

Suddenly the Ack Ack guns opened up, pumping shells into the sky. Black puffs surrounded the formation which made them break up.

Now, in came the Spitfires and Hurricanes weaving in and out with the rattle of machine guns.

An Officer came up to us: "Get in the slit trenches."

A young soldier said: "The bloody cheek of them coming over like that. At first, I thought it was ours."

As the enemy was returning home, one Heinkel was flying low with a Hurricane on its tail. We could see the crew as black smoke poured out of its tail. Then in the distance, a pyramid of smoke, as it hit the ground. And the long wailing of the All Clear siren. Sergeant Dilks called his team together. Ten young soldiers (average age 20) sat on the grass near the sign "The Times Sports Ground. Keep Off the Grass." From the large hut, they were restocking the shells for the guns.

Sergeant Dilks said five of us would stand by from eight o'clock until midnight and five midnight until dawn: two on the locator, two on the searchlight and one on the generator. The information from the RADAR on the locator moved the searchlight up, down and around without the beam, like a robot. The readings were relayed to the predictor on the guns.

The equipment was all ready for action as we lay on the grass again. The wail of sirens again. This time the German planes were high in the sky. We watched the vapour trails through powerful binoculars as our fighters weaved in and out of the formation following them out to the coast.

At night, the gunners, not being able to see the targets, put up a box barrage near the target. So the RADAR could pick up the enemy. Sergeant Dilks and I had a telephone breast set on to speak to the predictor linked by cable. The breast set hung on the chest so you could speak into it whilst leaving your hands free.

It was uncanny watching the searchlight moving as it followed the enemy planes without the beam on. I had a torch on my knees, the Sergeant read the angles and, after a few seconds, the guns were pumping shells at the planes overhead. Then the whistling sounds of shrapnel. It came down like rain after exploding around the planes.

At midnight the All Clear sounded. The Sergeant told the second team to take over.

An Officer said: "They will be back about one o'clock."

After a tea break, sure enough the sirens wailed again. At dawn, to our relief the All Clear sounded. After breakfast, the crews tried to get some sleep. But, by ten o'clock, another warning and the restocked guns were firing at waves of planes, and fighter planes were very busy machine gunning. The searchlight crew could do nothing but watch.

What was the Londoner doing, who was at the mercy of the bombs all night and now more bombs? Men had to go to work, shops had to open, people had to eat: there was no peace night or day. Every time the Air Raid warning sounded, a sickly feeling in the stomach.

Back on duty as night fell, the Sergeant and I were reading angles and bearings to the gunners when the sky started to light up as hundreds of bright flares slowly drifted across the gunsite. It was as if dawn had broken with daylight. All the planes above us could see us. You wished you could hide. We could see the slit trenches with cooks, office staff all cowering to get out of sight. The guns kept their barrage of shells going through the flares.

Next came incendiary bombs. Hundreds. Spread like confetti across us. The magesium burning fiercely. An Officer shouted for everyone to go and put sand on them. Some had dropped through huts. Everyone worked hard. The flares hit the ground. Darkness again and a sigh of relief as the All Clear sounded. There were heaps of cinders, like mole hills, where incendiaries had been put out. Small parachutes were scattered about from the flares, heaps of empy shell cases near the guns.

It was our first experience of war. We had just had breakfast and lying on the floor of the hut when the siren sounded again. Wave after wave of German planes came over.

The Sergeant asked me to go with a lorry driver to fetch a replacement for the RADAR. It was a big American lorry. You sat high in the cab. As we rode along, we saw the destruction the bombers had caused. We returned through Lewisham, a town like Nottingham, large shops just heaps of rubble, large steel girders just bent and twisted like hairpins still smouldering. A large housing estate flattened, just heaps of bricks.

Some Londoners were carrying suit cases and clothes: all they had left. When we pulled up, we asked about the bombing. One old chap said it was a landmine that had dropped on the estate. It was a huge cylinder bomb dropped on a parachute. As it dropped slowly to the ground, with the detonator under the base of the bomb, it exploded sideways, not making a crater. It caused blast to a large area. Soldiers and firemen were still digging for trapped civilians among the rubble.

As we drove across London, it was getting dusk. The pavements were full of people. Mothers and little tots, men carrying blankets, all making their way to the shelters in underground stations. Men who had worked all day now all set for a miserable night.

As we pulled back into camp, the wailing of sirens and the familiar sound of the German plane engines. I went with the Sergeant, first shift on, slowly reading information for the gun predictor as the searchlight moved slowly up and down to where the RADAR set it. The guns started pumping shells, shrapnel was falling.With a sudden blast, we were blown against the ammo dump, fire all around us. We started putting the fire out using our greatcoats.

The jagged edges of a steel cannister and thick oil pouring out. This oil bomb had set the field alight.

As the dust cleared, we could see one of the guns was on its side.

The gun position Officer was shouting: "Stick to your guns. Keep firing."

Someone answered: "Bollocks."

Suddenly there was a rush of air and a crunching sound as a stick of bombs dropped among the smoke and flames. We had been made a target by the fire. As the guns lay silent now, there were faint cried of: "Help."

We were covered in thick oil and made our way to a barrack hut. At the bottom of a large crater, the conrete base of the hut lay on trapped soldiers. As ambulances cleared the wounded and dead, dawn was breaking and the All Clear was a lovely sound to hear.

But the devastion: craters, guns tipped over, barrack huts smashed, lumps of turf, shell cases. Weary soldiers with black faces went to the cookhouse for breakfast. As we lay on the floor of our hut, you could see the clouds roll by, lumps of asbestos roof and grass sods around us. We fell asleep.

At midday a large explosion awoke us, with grass and earth falling on the site. It was a delayed action bomb. It blew the tennis courts to smithereens. No one injured. But glass and debris covered the site. Two new guns were brought on to the site and by night we were ready for the raiders again.

It was now December with cold nights. Sergeant Dilks told us to pack our kits. We were moving to a new site. The sirens sounded as we moved off. We were soon in the centre of London going towards docklands. Again, we were surprised at the ruins. We passed people trying to carry on, shops still open.

Signs saying: "Business as usual." Firemen and ARP bringing out dead from the rubble.

As we came to the East End, we could see giant cranes at the side of the Thames. We pulled on to Southwark Park, in Bermondsey, at the side of the Surrey Docks. The cranes were unloading large ships, vital food and materials, but there were lots of burnt out warehouses, bomb damage and rubble everywhere.

As we pulled our equipment to the side of the guns, we were looked at with suspicion. It was to be the same routine, reading angles and bearings. As dusk fell, the raids started. First, thousands of incendiary bombs set fire to the docks. The Thames looked as if it was on fire, the tall cranes silhouetted, and firemen in the thick of it. As a fire engine raced down the road, a bomb dropped in front of it throwing it into the air.

Then the second wave of planes carrying bombs came, like a moth to a candle, to unload into the flames. Houses near by were hit. Thick black smoke. Clouds of steam as water was poured on the burning buildings. The firemen were so brave, high on ladders, an impossible task. ARP and Ambulance men searched among the rubble for injured and dead. The All Clear sounded at midnight. Then more raiders. At one o'clock, some of the cranes were hanging down into the water: the heat was so fierce.

As we were about to change shifts, the gun position Officer told the Sergeant to expose the beam on the enemy. The gunsite was in complete darkness as the Sergeant shouted: "Expose."

In a split second, it was daylight as the powerful beam reached into the sky on to a plane as it weaved and turned as the shells burst around it. It dived to the safety of the darkness.

94

But now there was a near mutiny from the gunners.

They felt exposed to the enemy with the light on so near to them. Two bombs fell near the guns. Sergeant Dilks went over to the hut to tell our relief team to get into the slit trenches. As they dived into a trench, a stick of bombs dropped across the site. A corrugated ablution and toilet was peppered with shrapnel. It looked like a collander.

As our own shrapnel from the shells exploding overhead dropped like rain, we could see the ground covered with small pieces of white marble. It was from a direct hit on the park's paddling pool.

As we returned to the hut after breakfast, its door was hanging off and the roof split open letting the sunshine through. As we folded the blankets, we could see they were full of holes shredded by shrapnel that had stuck in the wooden floor and covered in broken glass. The five soldiers had left the hut just before the blast.

Now most of the German raids were at night. The months of day and night bombing had taken their toll on the nerves of civillians and the gunners, mostly through lack of sleep.

Joe and I were on second shift and asked if we could go for a walk around. A short way down a road, we saw a pub. As we entered, the air raid warning sounded. The place was packed, thick with tobacco smoke. We went to the bar and asked for two pints. The whole building shuddered, glasses dropped off the shelves.

The landlord shouted: "The cellar door is open if anyone wants to take cover."

But a Cockney started playing the piano.

Although the bombs were dropping, they carried on. As windows broke and dust came off the ceiling, they carried on singing.

As we went back to the site, the raid was very heavy. Sergeant Dilks said the site had a direct hit. By the light of the beam, we could see the guns tipped over. Over the craters hung a cloud of dust, but the beam was still searching for the enemy.

It is fifty-four years now since this happened. In the papers now people are saying we were wrong to bomb German cities such as Dresden because so many civilians died. But these people have no idea how the Londoner, and such cities as Coventry, had their guts bombed out of them. Hitler was to blame for the German people's sorrow. He didn't care where the flying bombs, the V1, and later the dreaded rockets, the V2, landed. As the bombs fell on London, Churchill said Germany would get it back ten fold and he kept his promise.

The regiment I was in was a London mob, the Middlesex Regiment, so two of them were allowed home at the weekend each week.

It was a big surprise when Joe and I were told we were going on leave for a week. We were given a railway warrant and set off to the underground station to get to St Pancreas for a train to Nottingham.

As we went down the steps to the tube it was an unbelievable sight. The platform was covered in people packed together, like sardines in a tin. As the train pulled along the platform, we had to step over them to board it. Imagine taking kids and blankets down there every night then out back home in the morning for school. Hundreds of kids were sent into the country to be safe from the raids.

Arriving in Nottingham in the early hours, an air raid warning sounded, so the buses stopped. I had to walk four miles home. The city I had left was being bombed to hell, but the trams carried on while the bombs dropped.

Back in London, as we came out of the tube we were told that a nearby underground had a direct hit on its entrance and it would take weeks to reach some bodies. Returning to Surrey Docks, our team was loaded up ready to move, this time to Abbey Wood near Woolwich Arsenal.

This site had large guns fixed to concrete bases and with concrete walls around them for protection. We could see the Dagenham Ford Factory, now making war materials.

On the new site, it was night time, the sirens had gone and the large guns were in action. Nobody wanted to know us. Sergeant Dilks asked an Officer for instructions.

He said: "I can't find you acommodation tonight, sleep in the lorries."

But you can't beat the British soldier for scrounging. The lads were soon looking around. Away from the guns was a long Nissen hut. I opened the door. Joe followed. The light came on when the door was shut. Suddenly the noise of the guns made the hut shudder. Row upon row of shell cannisters lay on the floor. It was an ammo dump. We told the Sergeant, and with our bedding settled on the cannisters.

Early next morning, we found the ablutions for a wash and shave, and the cookhouse for breakfast. Then, back in the ammo dump we were folding our bedding when in walked a man in a peaked cap with a badge on.

"What are you lot doing in here," he said?

"We couldn't find anywhere to sleep, so we kipped down here."

He started to laugh. "Do you know what you've been sleeping on. I hope you slept well," he said. "These shells are hospital cases." "What's that," I asked?

"These have been fired up the barrels but failed to fire," he told us. "The detonators have been struck by the firing pin but nothing happened, so they could go off anytime. The hut is placed out of the way!" So we grabbed our bedding to make a quick exit. Then we saw a sign "Dangerous Explosives. Keep Out."

The gun position Officer told the Sergeant there was no sleeping accommodation, so a Bell Tent had been erected near the guns. And there would be a full search light drill with the beam exposed on any target flying over. It was getting very cold: January.

This gunsite had a more modern RADAR system. It was very successful until in the light we saw thousands of thin strips of tin foil like Christmas tinsel. It fell all around us.

One Cockney said: "Has someone got married? It's like confetti."

The RADAR was hitting the enemy hard with plane losses. Dropping the metal strips upset our trace on the screens. The code for the strips was WINDOW.

One dark moonless night, the Officer came to us with a report that they were dropping Land Mines. "If you see anything, disperse beam and search." This means instead of the beam going into the sky, it is put out of focus to make a wide light.

We asked the Sergeant what we did if we saw one and he said: "Run like hell." I described one of these Land Mines earlier. On most raids now, there was WINDOW.

It was now around March 1941. We were so tired through lack of sleep, we could sleep through gunfire. Daylight raids had fizzled out and we had some raid free nights. Sometimes we heard planes high in the sky on the way to other cities. Sergeant Dilks decided to give us a break. In twos we were given passes for forty-eight hours in London. Joe and I were first.

We went on the tram. Woolwich was a military town with one of the largest ammo factories. In one very large crater, about thirty foot deep, we saw a bus. It looked like a toy thrown away by a child. I remember this leave very well. It started about 8.0 a.m. on a clear cold morning.

We walked over Tower Bridge and along the Old Kent Road. We were both amazed at the destruction. The civilians were in the battlfield. The rest of the country didn't know how bad it was because of restricted news. By midday we were in the centre of London. The Cenotaph in memory of the dead of the First World War, looked smaller than on pictures.

We visited Madam Tussauds wax works. It said: "Open." On the steps was a wax model of a commissionaire. As we passed, the model said: "put out the cigarette. No Smoking"

We went down to the Chamber of Horrors. On the way out, a frail old lady had fallen asleep. Her handbag dropped on the floor.

Joe said: "Wake her up."

I said: " No, she might be another model."

We went to The Strand. Soldiers of all nations strolling about. We came to the Union Jack Club, a posh hostel for servicemen. We booked in to come back for bed and breakfast. It was only a shilling. We sat in the lounge with a mug of tea.

Joe said :"You know your way about, where do you want to go?" For some reason, we went on a tram to the Elephant and Castle. I remember a large junction where all the trams met. During the day there were a few air raid warnings.

As it was getting dark, I said to Joe we should be getting back to The Strand. He said we were booked in and could arrive anytime in the night. There was a large pub on the corner with singing coming out. It was "The Elephant and Castle." As we went in, the sirens wailed.

"Let's go in here for a warm," said Joe. The piano was playing The White Cliffs of Dover.

"What do you want soldiers?" a buxom barmaid said. We took two pints to a big roaring fire at the end of the bar. As we started warming our hands, a fat old lady with her legs wide open said: "You can warm your hands up here, soldier." Suddenly the whole building shook. But no one panicked and carried on singing.

An old man came in and said: "That was a near miss." We were about to leave for The Strand when two girls came to us and asked if we wanted to go to a party.

"No," said Joe "We ought to get back to the Club."

"You might not make it with the raids on," I said. "When you are out you are out." With a few pints down us, we said "Yes."

"Well, bring two quart bottles each and follow us when we go," they said. With the Dutch courage in us, we followed the girls, a bottle in each hand. As they struggled along, the thump, thump of the guns.

"We are celebrating Mother's birthday," they said as they arrived at the bottom of some steps. "It's the top flat." We stuck together in case of trouble. The party was going strong with lots of girls, sailors, airmen. All brought bottles. Beer flowed. Joe was looking for a toilet. Along the corridor, the door was locked.

A big blonde said: "It's booked" as she straddled the sink. A powerful stream of hot liquid hit the sink. Pulling her knickers up, she said: "Hang it over here, soldier."

We sat on the settee watching one girl dancing to the music. Then slowly, she gave a strip-tease. Now and again the windows rattled with the bombs and guns. But we fell asleep. In the morning, bodies lay in all positions on the floor, beer bottles everywhere. We put on our greatcoats and said cheerio to the girls. We caught a tram and then walked the rest back to camp. It had been a break we needed and a good experience.

The raids were getting less. Again we were told to be prepared to move. But that night, an unexplained incident happened about a mile from us, a loud explosion. We thought it was a delayed bomb, but a few seconds after there was a terrific roar like an express passing over. That was a mystery.

The Sergeant told us it was a top secret. Hitler had a new weapon. It was a rocket missile. Then we solved the mystery. It travelled faster than sound, that came after it landed. This was to be a terrible weapon.

There was no defence against it. This explosion must have been one of the experimental V1 or V2's on London. Later on, the Londoners had to bear the brunt of these bombs. So when you hear how the Battle of Britain was won by the few fighter pilots, remember the lots of people who also won it.

April 1941, our convoy travelled back to the fields of East Anglia. The peace and quiet was uncanny after London. But we talked about the blitz on those lonely sites. We often thought of the people we had left to the fate of the new menace

By the beginning of 1944, there was little bomber activity over England. With the need for the British to get back into France, I was sent to retrain as an Infantryman. What a shock after my country life, back on the barrack square, marching and battle training ready for the Second Front.

After eight weeks in Colchester Barracks, I was in the Wiltshire Regiment attached to the 7th Gloucesters. A thing I hated as a kid, a fully trained infantry soldier ready to be mown down like the young men in the First World War. Our final battle training, to my surprise, was in Cromer in the Norfolk I loved.

One hundred men in this empty hotel on the coast. We received our rail warrants, and nine days embarkation leave pass to start next day Monday. Packing our kit Sunday morning, the door burst open.

The Sergeant Major said: "Private Cross and Private Smith. Follow me."

As we marched quickly with him, he said: "Look smart, the C.O. wants to see you. Left, right, left, right."

The C.O. said: "At ease. With the invasion into France, they took all the Army Catering Corps cooks. We have no cook in the Officers' Mess. And cooks are needed in the mens cookhouse."

Looking at me, he said: "Embarkation cancelled. You report to the Mess on Monday at nine o'clock."

I said: "Sir, I am only a Regimental Cook. I would sooner go with the lads I trained with."

"If you refuse, you are on a charge," he said.

And I was marched out and that's how I spent the rest of my Service. From the rough looking fully trained Infantryman straight off the assault course ready to go into war in Europe, I had to prepare meals, breakfast, lunch, teatime snacks and evening meal (sometimes seven course) at this private hotel, The Christian Endeavour Hotel, Overstrand, near Cromer. Seven days a week for seventyfive Officers and a Brigadier.

There was a staff Sergeant-in-charge, dressed in white, three gold stripes on his sleeve; eight grade three soldiers employed as batmen and waiters, and me the Chef, white trousers, jacket, apron and tall chef's hat.

The waiters served meals in white coats, preparing the tables with the hotel crockery and cutlery. The white tiled kitchen and larder was modern. The variety of food was improved by the Mess fees paid each week by the Officers. Fresh vegetables were brought daily, and eggs, from the local farmer.

My knowledge of cookery was improved by finding Mrs Beaton's Cookery Book in the larder. I complained to the Mess Officer that I was fed up working long hours seven days a week. So the Sergeant arranged for me to have Saturday evenings off from six o'clock. To do that, we had to put on a buffet meal for that night.

I had only been in the job a week. One evening as I was preparing to serve up the meal, a Sergeant and two soldiers marched into the kitchen.

"Are you private Cross, 902 728?"

"Yes," I replied.

"You are under arrest. Escort, take him out." As I was taking my apron off, in walked the Mess Sergeant and asked what the charge was.

" Failing to read Company orders, failing to report for Guard on three counts and Fire picket four times."

I thought this was the chance to get back to duty as a soldier.

The Mess Sergeant shouted: "You can't do this. All the Officers are in the dining room waiting for dinner. If you take him, it will be you three who are under arrest tonight."

They marched out and I carried on with the meal. I found out I had been reported absent without leave for weeks. No one knew where I was!

Saturday morning, in came a fisherman from the beach a few yards away wearing rubber waders, sou'wester and carrying a large hamper.

As he dropped it on the floor, he said: "It's paid for." I opened it. Crabs and lobsters crawling about!

I shouted back at him: "What do I do with these?"

"Boil them," he said and went off.

Mrs Beaton said put the live crabs or lobsters into cold water for a while to make them vomit to get the salt water out. I did this. The water went green. Then into boiling water, boil until bright red. I thought it was cruel as I heard the squeaks and cries as they boiled alive. I spent an hour cleaning them and dressing them for the buffet salad.

The following Saturday, the fisherman brought a large salmon. Again, with Mrs Beaton's advice, I gutted it, cooked it with its head still on. It looked good on a large meat dish on a bed of lettuce and tomatoes. The buffet was a success, served by the waiters. Hot soup, salmon or crab or lobster, salad, hot potatoes and coffee. The main thing: I had my night off.

One night, the Sergeant said that twentyfive Officers were coming on manoeuvres early the next day. They would want breakfast at five o'clock and haversack rations. Then an evening meal on their return. The Guard woke me at four o'clock and I had to sign his book in case I turned over and went to sleep again and said I hadn't been wakened.

For the sandwiches, it meant spreading nearly two hundred slices of bread. And I still had the breakfast to prepare. I had a good idea. Laying the slices of bread on the work top, I then melted the margarine to oil. Then I fetched my shaving brush, gave it a good wash and painted the liquid margarine on to the bread. It was a lot quicker than spreading. Then corned beef on and a slice on top. Two large sandwiches and a lump of Army cake in a bag: twenty five haversack rations made in half-an-hour.

Every day, I was sent two or three men called Janker Wallers (offenders). Their job was to peel spuds and wash dirty dishes. One night I was preparing the evening meal. The veg was late being delivered. I asked one of these men to wash and prepare the cauliflower. I had no time to soak it in cold water to clear the grubs out.

The meal had two servings of this vegetable. Cauliflower-au-gratin and, on the main course, cauliflower in white sauce. At the end of the meal, a waiter brought me a small card on a tray. It said "Compliments of the Colonel." On the tray was a large caterpiller. A minute later, he came again. The same complaint. The Brigadier had found one also.

Once a month, it was Officers' guest night. They had to dress in full uniform and could bring their wives and girl friends. Sometimes I had some thanks for a good meal. The waiters would bring me pints of beer with compliments from the junior Officers.

On my Saturday night off, I would borrow the caretaker's bike and cycle into the villages with some of the waiters. The routine was that after a few pints and the pub shut, we went to the village dance just in time for the last dance to the tune of "Who's taking you home tonight" or "After the dance is through." So you usually walked your partner home. To this day, I can still only do one dance, the Waltz.

On one such night out, I met Molly and we fell in love. I wanted to be with her all the time. She lived in a village near and came every night when I finished duty. We would walk along the cliffs in the moonlight by the sea. Around Christmas 1945, we had enjoyed two weeks together. I had been very busy with Christmas meals.

But sad news. The caretaker showed me a letter from the owners of the hotel. They were getting ready for opening again. The Army was moving out. Sure enough, in January we were told to pack to move off the next day. Molly was frantic and crying. I didn't know where I was going.

I said I would write and kissed her for the last time. The next morning, we marched to Cromer. We went by train to Crowborough in Sussex, a desolate camp. I remember the WVS gave out tea in jam jars: they must have lost a lot of cups an the trains.

I wrote to Molly every day. Then her letters stopped. Men were being interviewed for release. It was now 1946. I was 28 and it was my turn to go. I now had to start the second stage of my life.

THE STRANGE WAY BACK TO CIVILIAN LIFE

The war in Europe was over. Thousands of troops were to be programmed to return home. When my turn came, I was marched in front of the Colonel. He gave me compliments for being a good soldier, asking me not to leave the regiment but to sign on for seven or, even, fourteeen years. I said no.

Then he wrote me a reference to get a civilian job. A few years. later, this regiment The Gloucesters, were fighting in Korea with a loss of a lot of the men.

Two days later, after putting our blankets and rifle in the stores, we boarded a lorry and, with our kitbags, we travelled to Guildford. We were amazed! In this barracks, we had white sheets on the beds, a locker for clothes, the dining room had white table cloths on the tables. All this was to encourage us to sign on for more Army service.

A sergeant told us; "This is the Army of the future." They wanted us to stay and sign on. Next day we were on a train to York.

In a large aircraft hanger, there were row upon row of suits, overcoats, shirts. You could select your civilian outfit. I changed into my new selection. A raglan topcoat, a pin-stripe suit, collar and tie and brown shoes. In the mirror - from a soldier to James Cagney the gangster! I changed back to my uniform quickly, to be given a railway warrant to Bulwell, Nottingham.

Waiting on the station to come home, there were hundreds of soldiers carrying a cardboard box with their civilian clothes in. The wide boys, called Spivs, were offering £5 for the box.

On the train there was a feeling of excitement and then one as if you had lost something. After the greeting of homecoming, I looked around. The old kitchen table was still set with the medicine and tinned milk. There was the old black grate with the coal fire, the black kettle singing as the steam rose from the spout. In the scullery, pots and pans in the sink as I went for a wash. It was as if all this had been mothballed for seven years.

At night, Dad sat in his chair by the fire, Mother ironing. Still the old flat iron. My sister lived with us and her husband of a few weeks. She was expecting. Food was on ration. So they had their sugar and butter at one end of the table: ours at the other end.

I walked into Bulwell and called in the pub in my gangster outfit. I was a civilian now. The place was full of Polish airmen and the odd Yank. I felt out of place. I knew no one.

After one pint, the landlord shouted: "No more beer."

There was a rush to the door to find the next pub open. I followed the crowd. It was early, eight o'clock. A notice over the bar said "Closed at nine." Then I learnt the way of ordering, two pints (one in reserve) in case TIME was shouted. I was now missing my mates, looking at all the soldiers and airmen laughing and singing with the girls. I felt lonely and miserable. In my civilian outfit, I walked slowly home. I was a stranger in the town where I was born. They had all gone to bed. I sat near the fire. The radio was on. The war in the East had a long way to go.

I took my Army discharge paper out to read. It said I would be sent a draft of seventy pounds gratuity. I read my reference of seven years' service.

It said: "Employed as Officers' Mess Cook. Cheerful. Trustworthy. Reliable. Is an excellent cook." And I was going to take this to my old firm to start work again as a wood machinist at a builder's yard?

PART 4

SETTLING DOWN

WEDDING PLANS AND MY OLD JOB BACK

After a few weeks at home, I was getting bored. Nothing to do each day. I had been used to getting up at six o'clock, in the Officers' Mess, doing breakfast, lunch, tea and evening meal finishing at nine o'clock. Now I was going to the pub, at lunch and at night, for the company I missed. Within a month, my brother George came out of the Navy. This made the drinking worse.

So, one day, I walked to the builders for my old job back. The Manager welcomed me, telling me to start work as soon as I had settled down. I found I was a lot better at work. The firm had not changed: the steam engine, the boiler, and Percy Brown the undertaker was still putting the block of wood at the head of the coffins. I was back after seven years. Time had stood still. I was twenty-eight now. I had gone away just a boy growing up. Now I was a man, wanting a man's wage. The rate was three shilling an hour. £1.4s a day. With working Saturdays: £7 a week.

With working in Basford, I found I was attracted at night to the pubs. George and I met two bus conductresses in the Mason's Arms, Basford. We went out for a few weeks with them. Dot and Bet were out for a good time. Then I found out that Bet was married so I couldn't go with her. Her husband was in the Army, so I couldn't let him down. I told her so. George carried on seeing Dot. I found another girlfriend but she was only twenty years old.

I met George out one night. He was worried. Dot was expecting a child. He asked me what he should do. He was two years older than me, thirty.

I said: "Do you want to settle down?" He thought about things and decided to marry. But, with the housing shortage, he had to live with her parents. My young lady met someone her age. Now I was on my own.

At work now, electric motors took over from the steam engine, and modern new machines were installed. But wages never improved. There was also a bandsaw for cutting our own timber from the trees which were delivered by Bramleys on a tractor. I was very interested in the sawing and enjoyed it.

One night on my bus going to Basford, a girl spoke to me. I had known her when I was with the gang at sweet sixteen. We made a date. From then we started courting. Within a year, we decided to get married. I felt I wanted to settle down. Life was so different since the years away.

Money was always a problem. The first few weeks out of the Army, I had met a friend from when I worked at Raleigh. He had just come out of the Army. He suggested going to Australia. He wanted a pal to go with. It was only £10 Assisted Passage. But I declined, mostly because I had been away from home so long. I think in later years, I regretted not going.

What finally brought the wedding plans forward was that someone knew the owner of a small terraced house, coming up to let. My future bride and I went to see him.

He said: "You can have the key for £5." Nearly a week's wage to us. The shortage of houses was so bad, they could demand bribes for a tenancy. We were both working but were broke. I had not had a chance to save on Army pay but had a few pounds left from my gratuity.

We set a date, February 14th, Valentine's Day. We put the key in the door of our future house. It was a pigsty. It took me back to where I was born: a black fireplace, stone hearth, whitewashed walls, brick tiled floor. In the kitchen a stone sink, just a cold water tap and an outside toilet. A place fit for heroes to come back to! I had heard that somewhere before. History repeats itself.

Now the wedding day was fixed. We worked hard on decorating our little house. The black fireplace was black leaded, with a white stone hearth. Lino covered the floor tiles, with a carpet square on it. The scullery was very tiny. We put in a gas stove. Over the sink, we had an Ascot water heater.

We could not afford stair carpet. There was one medium size bedroom, one boxroom. Three outdoor toilets for six houses. But we had no furniture.

My Mother gave us her nearly new three-piece suite from her front room. Mother and Dad were on their own now as all the family had fled the nest. My sister and husband had a council house. I was the last to go.

As we were both working, we took out a hire purchase agreement to buy an oak dining table and chairs, a bedroom suite (bed, wardrobe, dressing table, tall boy). They were delivered and the house was ready before the wedding day. Now we were in debt to a total of one hundred and fifty pounds. A fortune for us to pay with £10 a week coming in.

February 14th, the wedding day, and I was dressed in a pin-striped suit, tailored at the Co-op. But when it was made, I only had enough coupons for three yards of cloth. So it was a bit tight.

The bride dressed in white silk because she knew somebody who worked in a factory and had brought some home in her shopping bag. Everything was still very hard to get. Rationing was very slow to come off.

I was marrying into a mining family, so they managed to get a good supply of drinks. Someone had killed a pig so there was plenty of boiled ham. There were about one hundred guests. As

Only this proof remains of the family wedding group outside Bulwell Parish Church. Back row left to right: Bill's Father: Rex (Joan's brother) Middle row: Bill's Mother; Bill's Sister-in-law Jean: Bill: Joan: Mavis (Joan's sister); Joan's Father and Mother.
Front row: Audrey (Bill's niece); Michael (Joan's brother)

we danced, some friends managed to get the keys to our little house to give us a surprise on our wedding night. We walked the short distance from the reception to our love nest.

As we entered, switching on the lights, nothing happened. No lights! I struck a match. The light bulb was on the table. I fixed it. We decided to go straight to bed. No lights again! As we stumbled about and fell on the bed, we found the bulb.

My new wife, Joan, had to use the chamber pot as it was a long way to the outdoor toilet. She let out a scream. The pot was overflowing with red froth. I thought just my luck on my wedding night.

As we settled in bed, everytime we moved there was a rattle of pots and pans. Tied to the springs were saucepans and baking tins! Our friends had fixed us up!

But next morning, some relatives of the wife took us to their house in Middlesex for a week's honeymoon. We really enjoyed London.

And so we started our married life. I was twenty-nine; the wife twenty-four. At last, I had settled down. But for the war, it might have been a lot earlier.

After the honeymoon, we found out the trick with the chamber pot was cochineal (red food colouring) and kayli powder put on the bottom of the chamber.

On the outskirts of Bulwell, where I was born, was Bestwood Village which was a mining community. Bestwood pit had been getting best steam coal from the Top Hard Seam for one hundred years. The coal faces were now four miles from the pit bottom. Over the years coal had been got in a radius of four miles.

In the 1930's, just before the Second World War, the mine had reached its limit. There were three reasons. First, safety. A fall of rock blocking the roadway could entomb men four miles from the shaft. Second, ventilation. It was getting hot underground through lack of air and air circulation.

Third, it was taking the miners about one hour to get to the coal face to start production. So the private coal owners decided to sink a shaft in the fields of the village of Calverton, a farming village four miles away from Bestwood pit. It had already reached Calverton on the coal faces underground.

The sinking started in 1937 at Calverton. But in this area the water supply is underground and pumped to Papplewick to supply Nottinghan with drinking water. The Bunter Sandstone held vast amounts of fresh water. As the shaft was sunk, the sinkers worked in terrible conditions up to their waists in water. Pumps worked day and night.

But the shaft was ready and workshops and baths built. When the war started in 1939 men came by bus to go down the shaft and were now at work at the face within minutes from getting off the cage. The ventilation improved. But the coal travelled on conveyor belts along the tunnels to Bestwood. At the end of their shift, the men came up the new shaft at Calverton, went through the baths and on the bus home.

After the war, the mines were nationalised. At Bestwood, it was decided to close the old Top Hard Seam going to Calverton, seal the shaft bottom and go higher up the shaft to open another seam, Main Bright.

At Calverton, it was planned to go for rich seams of coal under the farmlands around. To do this, another shaft had to be sunk at the side of No 1 shaft, through the water bearing strata again. It would give new life to the village and employ hundreds of people.

This is where my new life and work would start after my marriage in 1948. Fate was going to take me to be a miner. To sink the shaft, at least thirty fit young men were needed, ten on each of three shifts: days, afternoons, nights.

With the war just over, most who applied for the jobs were ex-servicemen whose trades were office workers, bricklayers, hosiery workers, shop assistants and joiners like me. All looking for a better paid job, mostly young men and just married wanting to settle down after the war.

I START AT THE PIT

We were both at work all day. My wife was working for a Nottingham lace firm. But after a meal, there was not much to do. No television in those days. Cinema was the main attraction. Then we called to see the family at their local on Saturday and Sunday nights. We joined family and friends in a sing-song with the piano playing.

It was still the war time spirit. Rationing was still on. Cigarettes were under the counter. There were still queues at the butcher for anything off ration such as liver. Clothing was still on coupons.

With the routine of drinking and smoking and living costs (although the rent was only four shillings and nine pence a week), instead of cutting down our expenses, I decided to look for a better job.

The friends we were keeping company with were miners with good paid jobs, including my father-in-law who was a Union offcial. It was a case of keeping up with the Joneses.

We went on the annual holiday for a week with this crowd and I was struggling counting my pennies when we returned.

Through my mining friends I was told they were to sink the new shaft at Calverton and they would want a sawyer.

One Sunday morning, my father-in-law took me to see his pit manager who was in charge of the Calverton sinking. He gave me the sawmill job.

At Hopewells the Builders, I put my notice in. The Manager was furious and said I must be in bad company wanting to work at a pit. But I wasn't going down the pit.

We liked the people in our community. Everyone was so friendly. There was an old public house in the village. It was like a farmhouse built in Bulwell stone. It was called the Coopers Arms. My wife had been a barmaid there. She was a family friend of the landlord's daughter, Marg, since school days.

The stone-built pub was like the village inns I had seen in Lincolnshire when I was in the Army. Narrow passages, low beamed, a large Tap room with a coal fire and bare wooden tables and quarry tiled floor. At the other end was the Snug room for select customers and the cricket team and gardeners. Gardening was the landlord's hobby. You paid a penny extra for your drinks to be brought to you in the lounge. There was a small stage at one end with a piano for entertainment.

The Monday I was to start my new job, I was to catch a bus at six o'clock to travel the five miles to Calverton to clock in at seven o'clock.

I had set my alarm for five, and as I walked with the miners, there were no pit boots on the cobble stones or ragged clothes to go to work in like I had seen as a boy. Now they looked as if they were going shopping. Most had a haversack and food in a tin (there were still mice in the pits).

Off the bus into the bright and warm bathhouse. The attendant gave me a key to a locker.

The system was, first to clean your locker. Then strip off and lock your clothes up. Walk naked carrying a towel and soap to your other locker, put on your working clothes leaving your soap and towel and go to work.

When you finished work, to your locker, put away the dirty clothes, now naked with towel and soap go to the shower, then to your clean locker, put on your suit and catch the bus.

118

FIRST IMPRESSIONS UNDERGROUND

At the Calverton pit, the enginewright-in-charge told me there was no sawmill. It was still to be built. They had ordered the circular saw. But he said: "We need a fitter's mate. Will you do that until the saw is fixed up?"

It was a large workshop, with lathes and drilling machines. I was introduced to Vin Jarvis. I was to be his mate. He was ex-Navy, and had been an engineer on a warship. I fetched and carried for him. He was making a steel platform to go in the new shaft.

It was a labouring job, no worries like the responsible job at the builders. We finished at two o'clock. I went through the baths, caught the bus and was back home: only three o'clock. It was strange being home so early.

Vin had told me that if I wanted another day I could work until six o'clock as he did.

He said you can work as much overtime as you want: "Some of us nearly live here."

So I stayed at work. My first wages, to my surprise was fourteen pounds, double my old wage. But I had worked Saturday and Sunday.

One special Sunday, I will never forget. I climbed up the ladder of the Coal Board lorry to sit in the back with the others (no bus at the weekends). Through the baths into my dirty clothes. In the workshop, Vin was waiting. He had a pit helmet on and a heavy miner's bucket lamp.

He passed me a helmet: "Put that on." I was shocked. He said: "The pump in Bestwood pit bottom has broken down. Bring my tools."

As the pit cage came to a halt, we stepped on. There was a rattle of chains as the gate came down with bells ringing. The cage dropped. My stomach came into my throat. The cage dropped at speed. Suddenly the cage pulled up. My stomach came back into my boots.

We stepped out into a large well-lit cave. A small railway track ran down the centre of a narrow roadway, with tree trunks each side holding girders across the roof. There were lumps of rock scattered around from the roof. Suddenly the road was blocked. There was a sound like water rushing. Vin got hold of a long metal handle attached to a door blocking the roadway.

He said: "Give me a pull." The noise stopped as the door opened. Then through another door into a large cave.

Vin explained to me they were airlock doors we had come through. Every pit has two shafts. One, where fresh air goes down travelling along the tunnels. It is pulled up another shaft as stale air and coal gas, methane. The air doors control it.

We came upon some brick buildings. We looked in. By the light of the lamp, mice scurried for cover. We were in the stables. Small pit ponies were munching oats, harnesses hung on whitewashed walls. They had mangers and brick floors.

We sat down on a bag of straw. I looked at my watch. Seven thirty, Sunday morning. I was three thousand feet underground. Fate had brought me to the pits I said I would never go into.

We carried on along a road turning right. We could see a bright light. Leaning against a steel pit tub (a box on wheels) was a tall man. He was bow-legged with a miner's safety lamp hanging on his belt. The long beam of a powerful spotlight on his helmet dazzled us. He carried a stick and was wearing a waistcoat with watch and chain. His shirt sleeves were rolled up. As he was

120

talking to us, he spat a stream of tobacco juice which shot over the pony's back.

He said to Vin: "Do you want a chew?" George offered him some black twist tobacco.

Vin said to me: "This is George Wesson, the Deputy in charge of the mine. By road Bestwood pit was about four miles away. But underground, we were going to it by tunnels as the crow flies, George said.

"When you get into this tub, keep your eyes on me. When I bend my head into the tub, you do the same or you will get your head knocked off by low girders," he said.

We sat cross-legged on our boots behind each other, our heads just above the tub. George's beam shone over the pony's back into the blackness. I could see pit props flying by, like sitting on a train watching telegraph poles flying by.

The tub was rattling and swaying. I could see the pony going up and down. As its ears touched the roof, it lowered its head, using them as a guide to where the roof was. Suddenly the pony stopped.

George said: "Who's going to open the doors then? It was air doors again. I squeezed out between the top of the tub and the roof.

Then this frightening journey started again. We came to a crossroads, a junction of five roads, but George carried on. I could see lights as we came out of the tunnel. It was like pulling into a railway station. As high as your lounge at home, it was Bestwood pit bottom.

We walked to the shaft. There was a fence across. As water ran down the shaft sides filling this huge well, it was about thirty feet deep. As we stood repairing the pump it was like being in a great shower. Vin soon had it working. George Wesson said it would take about two hours to get the water down to a safe level. We followed him to a brick cabin with tables and bench seats. We sat down looking through a window at a large working area where all the coal had come from the tunnels to go up the shaft.

Suddenly a telephone rang out. Yes, they had a telephone system all over the pit.

"They say you have to go back to Calverton, urgent," said George. "I can see to the pump. You will have to walk. I want the pony. Keep following the railway lines and if the ventilation is hitting your face its the right way."

Vin explained why we had had to travel all this way underground to Bestwood. They had sealed their bottom of the shaft. Now they were in a seam higher up. So their cage could not go down to the pump that had broken down.

MY FIRST ALLOTMENT GARDEN: 1949

That was a Sunday to remember all my life.

On the way back, we passed a row of brick buildings. Looking in, they were empty stables with about twenty mangers. So when this seam was in production, there must have been all these ponies bringing coal in tubs to go up in the shaft.

Vin led with the lamp. I was carrying the tools and sweat was running off my forehead. It was uneven walking. We clambered over heaps of rock that had fallen out of the roof. Dangerous lumps hanging from the roof could fall at anytime. Suddenly we came to a dip in the road and a glimmer of light. But it was the reflection of our lamp on water. Vin said we were lost.

We walked along a conveyor belt that had taken coal along the roads. We were wet now with sweat. We came to the junction of the five roads and the rail line and followed it back to Calverton. We came through the air doors into the pit bottom and to the cage to take us up. It was twelve o'clock as we sat in the workshop with a cup of tea.

How nice to be back in the fresh air. It was three o'clock when we finished work.

I didn't want to be a soldier, but fate changed that. Now I had been down a mine, but would I become a miner?

I was working seven days a week, but I used to like walking along the country lanes. One day, I stopped to talk to a nice old lady standing at her gate. Her house was built in stone like a mansion. She owned the land and the stone quarries.

I admired some sweet peas growing near her door.

"Are you interested in gardening," she asked.

"Yes," I said. "But I live down the road, only a back yard, no garden." I spoke to her often and she knew my wife.

Then one day, my wife said: "Mrs Reid wants to see you." As I went for my walk, she was at the gate.

"I have a garden to rent, " she said. "It's at the side of the quarry.

She gave me the keys to go and have a look. The hedges were high and I could not see over. But when I opened the gate, it was like a secret garden. Through a small orchard and a small piece of land, I could hear water. As I walked toward it, it was a stream full of water cress. Then I heard a splash as if someone had thrown a stone. Then another. It was trout jumping for the May fly.

Over the stream was another garden running up to the Coopers Arms pub, I went back to see Mrs Reid and to thank her.

She said: "It will be three pounds a year rent." I was so excited. I paid her in the old fashioned way.

She said: "Come in and I will give you a receipt."

I took to my new job easily and soon settled down. I suppose it was because of Army life, always moving. Getting up at five o'clock was very hard, especially if we were late going to bed after being out drinking with our friends. If I didn't do overtime, I was home at three o'clock and then I enjoyed the new garden.

I called it my secret garden. This was my bit of England. When you bolted the gate, you could relax, sit and have a cig., watch the kingfisher in its bright colours, or the dragon flies and the splashing of trout.

The landlord of the pub, Ernie Coleman, came into his garden across the stream. He told me the best place to grow kidney beans. It was at the side of the brook, easily watered.

Then he said: "If you put a plank across the stream, you can come through my orchard when you feel like a pint."

Another gardener along the stream, with a house and stables, told me to fetch some horse manure whenever I wanted. Such friendly people. I was getting to know the locals. Going just down the road was another public house, the Cross Keys. Just behind this was the blacksmith and the undertakers where, as a boy, I had taken the horse to be shod.

I looked around to remember. The forge was shut down, given way to the motor car. Next to the pub was Barber Bill, sixpence for a shave, a shilling for a haircut.

This shop was still in a time warp. You sat in an old fashioned beech chair for your haircut. He did it just with scissors, opposite a coal fire and the mantle piece. A clock chimed the time. A lad was lathering a man's face. My memory went back again to when I was a boy.

A little further do⁣⁣n the road was a general shop. I went in for cig's. Brass scales on the counter with small metal weights. The smell of soap, then bacon and cheese. Wall signs still advertising Reckitt's Dolly Blue for white clothes, and Coleman's Starch.

The shopkeepers, man and wife, looked about eighty. Around all the miners stone houses were sturdy stone walls. I could see why. There was a deep large quarry now full of water with reeds, cray fish, trout and gudgeon, water hens and coots. The stone for walls and houses came out of the quarry.

It was 1949, but I realised this small neighbourhood could have started in the 1800's. Everyone was so friendly, stopping to speak to you. During the war, I was told a lot of miners kept a pig in the back garden, and I noticed the local pubs all had stables and a built-in pig stye.

With better wages and the wife working, our debt for furniture was nearly paid. I was still working seven days a week. One Sunday, I caught the lorry at seven o'clock in Bulwell.

Vin said: "It's a big day to-day. Rope capping."

PART 5

MINER

ROPE CAPPING

Vin explained to me that by law the ends of the wire ropes have to be recapped and inspected, say, every month. The ropes hold the cages and take the strain of lifting the cages of about fifty tons, day and night, lifting tubs of coal and miners up and down the shaft.

The winding rope from the engine house goes over the head stock wheels, down to the cage. The end is coupled by pushing the one-inch round wire rope through a cone-shaped coupling iron, like pushing it through the base of an ice-cream cone. The steel wires are then splayed out in the cone, and hot metal poured onto the wires in the cone. When cold, the wires cannot pull out. From this cone, four heavy chains go to each corner of the cage.

It was very interesting to uncouple the rope from the cage. First a tub with a long girder on it was pushed under the cage and the cage lowered onto it, which let the heavy chains drop onto the cage roof. The same operation is done to the cage at the shaft bottom.

While the rope is being capped, the four heavy chains that held the cage are put in a furnace to burn off the grease. It was burnt off to clean the links to look for cracks in any link before the chains are put back on. It is very important because miners lives could be lost through faults.

It was while we were doing this, I saw another device which saves lives. It was called the Kings Patent. Years before my time, when the cage was being brought to the surface, it sometimes overshot the pit top, the cage hitting the headstocks, the rope breaking and the cage dropping down the shaft killing miners.

The device, at the top of the headstocks, was bolted on two inch thick steel plate with a twelve inch diameter hole. The winding rope went through this. On the rope near the cage was a scissor device, the centre of the scissors held by a copper pin. If the cage overwinds at the pit top, the scissors get pressed going through the hole in the steel plate and the copper pin gets cut. The scissors cut the rope which flies off the wheels, the cage drops with the scissor handles resting on the plate so the cage cannot drop down the shaft.

This actually happened at Calverton No 1 shaft. The rope fell into the pit yard and the cage hung in the headstocks with miners still in it. They brought the miners down from the cage by ladder. I hope this is not boring but I'm trying to explain an ingenious way of saving lives.

The capping took all day. Any mistake would cost lives. The shaft was inspected every day. The lorry came to take us home. It was seven o'clock.

A long busy day.

DANGEROUS WORK

Although I was working seven days a week, earning an average of seventeen pounds, we still could not save money in the bank. We had good clothes and food. It was always a good hot dinner every day, not like the present day frozen and microwave meals on a tray watching television. We still had the traditional Sunday dinner.

We also had a fortnight at Bournemouth every year. We lived well, but it was still a poor wage for the dangerous and uncomfortable working conditions.

But, now in my retirement, we can see we should have been prepared and cut out smoking and drinking so much. There was no superannuation scheme to pay into and that one annoyed me.

The white collar workers on the Coal Board, if off sick, were paid wages during illness. But, the miner whose chances of injury or sickness were more likely in the dangerous work, only received National Health sick pay.

I don't blame the office staff. It was the system. They also received a ton of coal a month free, like the manual workers, and a superannuation for retirement.

Thirty years later, all these benefits did come to the miner, but it was too late for thousands of workers.

Some of these dangerous jobs, I didn't like but you could not refuse when it was pushed onto you, like the one of greasing the ropes in the shaft.

Late one Sunday, going to the baths to get changed to go home, the enginewright said: "Can you come back and do me another job. I forgot the ropes want greasing."

I followed Vin into the stores. We came out dressed like men from outer space: a bright yellow oil skin suit, wellingtons, a leather harness on our waist and shoulders, with chains hanging. And a helmet with a shield at the neck. We had a large bucket of thick black grease each. We walked like this to the pit cage. The onsetter rang the Winding House to tell the driver what we were about to do. The cage came up but stopped at the heavy chains holding the cage.

"Right," said Vin, "be very careful."

He stepped among the chains and I passed the buckets and a miner's lamp. Then I carefully walked on.

"Clip your harness to the chains in case you fall off," said Vin laughing.

Bells rang. We dropped at speed, a lump in my throat. The brick wall flashed by. As we slowed down, I could see lights. It was pit bottom. Vin spoke.

"As the cage will go up very slowly now, you take that side and slap the grease on the ropes."

The ropes went through shoes on the cage, to guide it and stop it swinging in the shaft. I could see now why we had oilskins on and a shield on the neck. As we rose slowly it was like being under a waterfall.

What a relief to get off at the top! We washed our hands in paraffin and took the kit back to the store, then to the baths and home on the lorry. Seven o'clock again!.

We were now settled down to married life and we talked about having a family. My brother, George, ex-Navy, was breeding fast, and my sister had two, a boy and a girl. So we planned to have a baby.

A friend of the family kept a sweet and ice-cream shop, Cheethams. He was a comic. He started it on Commercial Road where miners passed to go to work at Shonkey pit. Wages were still low.

Some of them called every morning for tobacco for chewing or cigs and 'put them on the slate' (credit) and then pay out of wages. He built the business up and started making ice cream at a small factory behind his house.

There was plenty of opportunity to start your own business. You needed small capital. I look back now and wish I had taken a chance to open a cafe. I had the know-how. Or even a chip shop. But I stopped in the rut at the pit.

Cheetham, nick-named Chobber, was a good friend of the wife's family. I was passing his shop coming from work. He spoke to me.

Then he said: " Could you give me a hand to carry this hamper in the shop."

He was laughing and joking. As he lifted the lid, it was full of joints of beef. He lifted a freezer lid and the freezer was full of bags of sugar. He thanked me for the help and gave me a joint and a bag of sugar. Black Market! It was still very active years after the war.

At Christmas, Chobber and my father-in-law organised a neighbourhood party over the Co-op. It was one pound a head. All wives and children came and there was dancing and singing.

All the children were given presents (bought from Chobbber's shop); beer and spirits from the local pub. But, although it was good fun, it was a business venture for Chobber.

I met his brother George at the party. He had just left the Army. We talked about the war. We became good drinking pals, and he started working for his brother in the shop.

My in-laws' local was the Red Lion. Every Saturday and Sunday we met them and their friends. It was an expensive way of life. On top of that, smoking! It was a mug's game.

Closing time was ten o'clock but when the landlord shouted: "Time Please," we stayed behind in the small room after the customers left because the family were friends of the landlord. We would stay in the snug room until after midnight. Some who had been drinking beer would go on to Whiskey.

The landlady or landlord never bought a drink. They were making the profit and getting free drinks.

The funny thing about the Red Lion was that it was opposite the Bulwell Police Station so we had to sneak out of the door quietly after midnight.

The worse thing was that I had to be up at five o'clock to go to work.

A NEW JOB AT THE SHAFT: 1949

I had been at Calverton nearly one year. During this time, teams of men had sunk the new pit to a depth of sixty foot. A twenty four foot diameter hole in the ground. The circular walls were built in brick. The tall headstocks were over one hundred feet high. From the powerful electric winding gear, two ropes came over the headstock wheels to drop into the shaft.

The first sixty foot down had been dry, just going through the earth crust. But to go deeper, there was a serious problem. It was Bunter Sandstone with under ground lakes of water between the strata.

When the old shaft I had been working in had been sunk in 1937, although pumps were going day and night, men were working waist deep in water.

This new sinking had to go through the same water bearing strata. A German idea was to be used: to freeze the strata to a depth of four hundred yards through the water. This should stop flowing into the workings. Work had been done toward this.

A circle of holes had been drilled around the circumference of the shaft and four hundred yards deep through the water bearing sandstone. Pipes were put down and coupled in order to set up a freezer plant.

Now the sinking of the next sixty feet was to go on. I was called to the engineer's office. It had been decided to start sinking on three shifts: nights, days and afternoons.

Each shift had eight sinkers and a chargeman. Included, there had to be an engineer fitter and his mate to maintain compressed air drilling and boring machines, plus building the cast iron steel

SKETCH OF CALVERTON SHAFT SINKING 1948

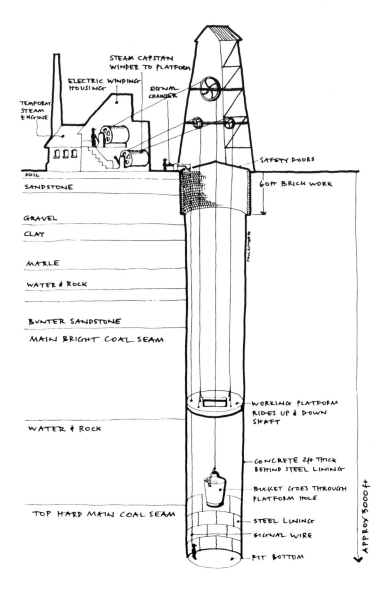

Drawn by Paul Rutter from a sketch by Bill Cross.

First team starting work on the segments to steel line the shaft at Calverton 1949
Top row left to right: Len Watson, Bill Cross, Danny Ancliffe.
Bottom row: Jack Hathern, Eddy Smith, Sam Whitehead, Arthur Miller.

casing with two feet of concrete behind it to hold back the water when the shaft thawed out.

I was to be mate to fitter, Sam Whitehead. My first shift was on nights.

Two large bucket shaped skips which could hold about thirty tons of rock were used. The winding rope was clipped on to a bucket handle and lowered down the shaft with the team of men in. At the bottom, the clip was taken off. The rope went back up the shaft. While they were filling the skip with rock, the other skip was lowered above their heads. When the first bucket skip was ready, the clip was transfered from the empty bucket to the full one. Thirty tons of rock went slowly up the shaft.

The danger was that a lump of rock falling down the shaft would gain speed and kill someone at the bottom. As safety against this, automatic compressed air doors closed when the skip arrived at the top, sealing the shaft off. The rock was tipped into a dumper truck, and the air doors opened to let the bucket down to be filled: a relay system as the rock was brought out.

The sinkers wore thick clothing with string vests to keep the heat in. It was like working in a freezer. Looking at the rock wall in the strata, the layers of ice would have been water pouring in the shaft had it not been frozen.

We had to go down four hundred yards through the frozen rock. On the ground near the headstocks were hundreds of curved iron segments, all numbered, ready to be lowered down to us so they would, like a jigsaw, make a circle of steel.

On my first shift, it seemed uncanny.

As I walked into the workshop the engineer came to me and said: "I have a shaft inspection. Come with me."

The shaft had to be inspected each time before the sinkers started work. We climbed into the large bucket. We had powerful electric light from a cable to follow us down, also a steel plate and hammer for signalling.

As we were slowly lowered, the cold hit us. It was freezing. As we looked at the rock walls, the ice glistened like bright diamonds. We had to look for loose rocks that could fall off the shaft side on to the men working in the confined space at the bottom.

Before our eyes was evidence of how the earth's crust was formed thousands of years ago: grey rock with fossils of mussel-like prints. Further down a two foot layer of gravel, probably a bed of a river. Then a two inch layer of coal, jet black against the other colours of brown marle-like clay.

We were going through earth where no man had been before. As we neared the bottom, the engineer hit the steel plate with the hammer. The bucket stopped. It was deathly quiet. Two hits on the plate. The sound echoed up the shaft.

Slowly we moved up. The signals, though a bit primitive, were the only way. Three to lower; one to stop; two to go up.

As we came out of the bucket, it felt quite warm in the night air.

To start off this jigsaw of steel, the chief engineer, the head surveyor, head fitter, two sinkers, fitter and fitter's mate all clambered into the bucket and unloaded on the shaft bottom. We all stood in the bright arc light as the bucket left us to go back.

The signals to the driver in his winding house were sent to him from the top of the shaft by electric button by the onsetter. But the signals from the shaft were very primitive: a wire rope from a clanger (a large hammer on a lever) at the pit top.

When the chargeman in the shaft pulled the wire rope, the hammer hit a steel plate on the shaft top. The number of hits was then relayed on the buttons to the winder.

As the surveyor, with spirit levels and tapes, was measuring, this huge dark shadow hung above us. It was the first segment, to start the jigsaw, as we lowered it into place. A thought hit me, if anything had gone wrong, we had no means of escape, no bucket on the rope.

FIRST CIRCULAR SEGMENT
TO LINE THE SHAFT 1949

Someone took a photo at the start of this dangerous venture. One thought! We were working in the dry through the invention of freezing, although it was very cold.

That night we laid a circle of kerbs to start lining the shaft. It was six o'clock. We all piled into the bucket, nine very cold men. We rose slowly as the chargeman pulled the wire rope and the two clangs echoed down the shaft from the clanger.

As we came into the morning air, it was very warm to us. Into the baths and a red hot shower, into clean clothes and on the bus home.

Nineteen Fifty! My life was so full with my job and my garden. I also did the odd joinery job. Looking back, I often wonder how I found the time with working seven days a week. My parents were getting very old.

My Father, at seventy-four, was still working as a builder, climbing ladders and scaffolds. I suppose he was of a breed like his father who was working up to his death at over eighty.

I have a theory about this. I think, with good health, counting out car accidents or serious illness, you live to the age of the parent you take after. My eldest brother, Tom, lived to eighty-one. I am seventy-six, still going strong. My sister's seventy-three. We all took after Mother.

There's one exception, brother George. He died at sixty two. His family was fifteen children with three sets of twins. Although he was a good worker in the lace trade, a twisthand, like a lot today he found that with Social Security he could get more money at home. That gave him time to drink all day.

He was a cheerful, comic character. The odd times he came to see me we would go for a pint. I asked how the family was.

He said : "Dot has had the operation, so she won't be having any more kids."

I said: "That's good."

He replied: "It's a bit late. Like shutting the stable door when the horse has bolted!"

Most Sundays we went to see my ageing parents. We were surprised to find George's eldest two boys living with them.

My Mother said: "Dot has a lot on." So the boys were going to the local school. My Dad was such a nice man, he agreed.

One day my parents were told their house was going to be sold.

The landord said: "I have found you another house in the next street." When she was settled in, we went to see her. I felt very sorry for them. They were back to a house exactly like the one I was born in and our family was brought up in.

Right from her childhood, my Mother had wanted a nice home. Now they were back to square one, with my brother's two boys to bring up. History was repeating itself for them. Tom had a row with George because he said he was putting on Mother. When Tom or I visited them, we always took some food and a small amount of money to help them. But Tom said George should take the responsibility and stopped going.

One night I found twenty Woodbine cigs in a drawer.

I said, joking: "Have you started smoking, Mother?"

She said: "I've got them for George, he never has any money."

A pensioner buying his cigs and bringing his kids up. Then I was disgusted with him. But a mother is always a mother, no matter what age you are. He was still her little boy.

Now at work on three shifts. I seemed to have more leisure time. Off night shift at seven o'clock, I would go to bed until twelve noon, then walk to the garden, over the plank into the pub for a pint, then back to do some digging or setting. Then home for the wife coming home, have tea, then two hours sleep before catching the bus for the night shift.

Afternoons: up at seven o'clock, see the wife off to work, do odd jobs, then to the garden, back home for dinner, catch the bus for one-thirty. I wasn't back home until eleven-thirty.

Days: early rising at five thirty, bus at six o'clock and back home at two thirty. After a brief rest, gardening again. Have tea when the wife came home. Nine o'clock, a walk to the Coopers Arms to join my friends.

This was my routine for years. The Coopers Arms should have been called the Gardeners' Rest. It was nearly all miners, mostly gardeners, in the tap room thick with tobacco smoke.

There was a large coal fire. Above the mantle piece, the dart board. There were old pine tables and miners playing 'tip-it': a button in one hand, with hands behind the back, move the button from hand to hand to hand, bring both closed fists in front of you, then your opponent has to guess where the button is.

Dominoes was the most popular game. Like footbacll, we played home and away at other pubs.

My wife's family lived in a fairly large house with a big garden. She had a younger sister, Mavis who worked as secretary for the Editor of the local paper. And a brother, Rex, a bit younger and another brother, Michael, twenty years younger. Rex was married just after ourselves.

We were still hoping to start a family. The wife decided to have tests and, if that was not successful, then I would have to see a doctor.

Chobbers brother, Ron, who was married, owned a house at Mablethorpe near the sea. The whole family plus friends hired it for a week. George Cheetham, Chobber's brother went also. We had good weather. But, again, with such a large crowd, it was beer drinking and parties, and I was broke again.

So I needed a well paid job to keep up with the Joneses and the work in the shaft would soon be complete. I think the reason I was so friendly with George was that he was like the mates I had in the Army. When we were out drinking, he was like my Army pals. But I was often in trouble with the wife for being out late and a bit unsteady.

ACCIDENT AVOIDED

The cast iron sleeve through the bunter sandstone was now complete. The sinkers carried on going down through the rock to reach the seams of coal, Top Hard. When this was done, it would be up to the miners to tunnel and mine the coal. The safety had been good, but one young man had lost his life falling off the scaffold and sixty feet down to the rocks at the bottom of the shaft.

The finish of the steel lining through the water bearing strata. Note the numbers, as the 'jigsaw' is complete.

Within weeks of the shaft thawing out, I went on shaft inspection with the engineer. As we slowly dropped down, water was coming in and running down the shaft. Through some of the iron segments, at the lead joints, water was shooting across the shaft. We reported it to the Master Sinker, Cyril Wesson, and he said it was impossible to make a watertight shaft. The pumps to be installed at the pit bottom would control it.

But he said the jets of water shooting across would have to be 'corked'. They are called 'pissers.' I can understand, that's what they looked like. It was to be done on a Sunday night shift by our team. I caught a lorry in Bulwell at nine o'clock that night. Then, into the baths and into working clothes.

As I was going to the pit top, someone said: "They are all in the canteen."

As I opened the door of the wooden hut, the sinkers in work clothes sat at tables, pints of beer flowing. It was someone's birthday. They gave me a pint. The place looked like Klondike in the Gold Rush with thick tobacco smoke.

It was ten o'clock, time to go down the shaft. As we all clambered into the bucket, Alf Curtis, the onsetter, passed us hammers and chisels to knock the lead back into the joints to stop the 'pissers.'

As the bucket dropped down the shaft through the pisser jets of water, the chargeman hit the iron plate to signal stop. We stopped at the scaffold and, pulling the bucket to the side, we climbed on to it. Working on the platform, we hammered away, sealing the joints. It was like working under a shower.

We had to raise the platform up to do some more work. As we prepared to move, the rule was to stand and watch the scaffold did not snag on pipes on the shaft side. The platform moved, but was held fast at one side by a pipe. The chargeman was hitting the plate to stop. But the scaffold was tipping us off. The bucket was still there.

He shouted: "All in the bucket."

We scrambled in as the platform tipped right up, then stopped. He hit the plate twice and we were brought out. There were arguments and nearly fights. The onsetter had been pressing the wrong button on the pit top. Some were blaming the drinking and some blaming the button man. Tempers were frayed and it was frightening. There was an enquiry and he was sacked. We had nearly been killed.

But I think the beer drinking had a lot to do with it. Everything had dropped off the platform on to the rocks 200 feet below.

We were very lucky we were not at the bottom of the shaft also.

Good news! My wife, Joan, was expecting (1952). All the family was excited as we prepared for the happy event. But life went on as usual. She still wanted to go to work. We still met the family and friends. We reckoned the happy event was due in Februrary 1953.

The sinkers were to finish in about one month, then the miners would take over to make the coal face. Another shaft was to be sunk at Cotgrave to start a new mine. They would use the same team that had done so well. Old pits were closing up North, and redundant miners would be paid to move to Nottingham to man the new pits. I was asked to move to work with the sinkers on the new shaft at Cotgrave. But, now, with a baby expected, it would be a lot of travelling time, and working all hours.

I was told the sawmill was now ready, the job I had come to the mine to do. I decided to stay. My last shift before going to sawing was an eventful one. Sam and I were wanted in the shaft to fix another pipe on the ventilation to get air to the workers. The shaft had reached a great depth. We took the pipe and tools down in the bucket. The noise of compressed air-drills echoed toward us from the bottom.

We bolted the pipe on. Then the shotfirer said: "Everyone up the shaft, I am going to prime these holes."

But he said to Sam: "Can I borrow your mate to help. The sinkers are going to have their snap." Up they went.

It was quiet now but for the dripping of water and the revs of the pump on the scaffold above us. From a box of explosives, he said: "Put four sticks down each hole." There were about fifty holes that had been bored six foot down into the rock. On the final stick of explosive for each hole, the shotfirer pushed in a detonator, completing each one by sealing it with clay, leaving two wires sticking out. All the wires sticking out from the detonators from each hole were coupled up to make a circuit. The last two wires were fixed to a cable coming down the shaft to make an electric circuit.

Picking up all the tools and the light, we climbed into the bucket. Hitting the plate, we then rose to the top. It struck me then that I had been standing on a massive amount of explovise, a large bomb.

In the brick cabin sat the sinkers with a big coal fire (the coal had come out of the shaft). The shotfirer coupled the cable from the shaft to a battery detonator.

He went outside shouting: "Fire, Fire!" Then he wound a small handle. Silence for a second, then the earth moved like a small earthquake.

The brick cabin shook. Within minutes, clouds of smoke came out of the shaft like a volcano. It would be half an hour before anyone could go down the shaft.

Turning to me, the engineer said: "Bill, do me a favour. While these men are having their snap, take this grease. The headstock wheels need greasing."

I thought he was joking. Nearly two hundred feet up! I couldn't be chicken in front of the team. I climbed slowly. At the top, out of breath, leaning on the safety rails, I looked down. Not only was I nearly two hundred feet up, I was also looking down the shaft.

When I came down, the shotfirer said: "Come with me to inspect the shaft." As the bucket descended slowly, we looked out for anything that could drop down on men below. He hit the gong. We hung over huge lumps of rock the sinkers had to clear.

The next day, I was at my new job in the sawmill. I was using the saw as if I had never been away. How quick life can change! I still think life is planned out for each person. In the Army, I missed the danger, being moved to the cookhouse. I had been in danger again, now I was safe in the sawmill, unless I cut my fingers off.

But had I made a mistake? Within a month, all overtime had stopped. No weekend working. And a baby on the way. My wages dropped. To be fair, the engineer made a roster out for overtime work, but I was never on it. A comical thing happened.

I was in the workshop talking to the blacksmith at his forge when he said: "Just watch this." One of the labourer's who lived in the village came to the engineer's bag hanging on a nail near the office. He looked round, then put a parcel in it. We waited, then went to have a look. A piece of pork and a dozen eggs! Most of the villagers kept pigs and poultry.

"That's how to get on the roster," said George. Then he took a few eggs out and, over at the forge, we boiled them for ten minutes then put them back with the others.

"I should like to see his face when he tries to crack one in the pan," said George. The man <u>wasn't</u> on the roster for a while.

After six months, I was told that, at Bestwood, they urgently needed men on the conveyor belts bringing coal out, with lots of overtime. So from Calverton, I transfered to Bestwood. It was the most boring work I had ever done, walking along the pit tunnels watching the coal travelling out in case a belt broke. I then had to mend it to keep production going.

To keep up with the Joneses again, I applied to go as a miner on the coal face which would double my wage and also break my second vow again, never to be a miner.

BIRTH OF OUR DAUGHTER

Saturday 14th February 1953, St.Valentine's Day, was the fifth anniversary of our wedding and the day our baby daughter was born. A double celebration.

In the morning, Joan had some terrible pains, walking around the room holding her tummy. But, looking at her, you could not tell she was expecting. She was still slim.

I phoned the midwife.

On looking at all the greeting cards, she said; "Right, we are going to have this baby born on your anniversary." She left but came back at tea time with her tools. I asked if I could do anything.

She said: "You have done enough, keep out of the way."

The wife was now in bed. I sat at the bottom of the stairs, listening.

She shouted: "Go, phone for gas and air." A man came in a car. I took it up, and went back on the stairs.

About nine fifteen, I heard the baby cry. I also cried with joy.

"You can come up now," she said in a stern voice. What a lovely scene! Brightly decorated bedroom, fire burning in the little black grate, the new cot ready for the baby and Joan had her in her arms. A little girl: Pamela Jane Cross.

It was nearly ten o'clock, I was to get the doctor to come and check if Joan might want stitches. After phoning her, I called in the Cross Keys to tell her mother and father and knock back a much needed pint. The locals cheered and congratulated me.

It had been arranged for Aunt Nance, a maiden Aunt, to look after things. She had been a nursing sister. I should go to work. Her mother and dad came to see their first granddaughter the same night.

But when Aunty took over, she said no visitors for two days. This caused disappointment in the family, but I suppose she was right.

On Sunday, Aunty did the dinner then told me to go and celebrate. I walked through my garden over the plank... It was too cold to garden. What characters. Jacky Shaw, with his clay pipe smoking the place out. I am sure he smoked privet hedge clippings. Polly came in with a pot jug, a beret on her head, bib and brace pinafore, her little dog at her heels. Jack Walker, the village ram. He lived up the lane with his widowed mother; the cockney still with a London accent; my best pal, George Cheetham, who wanted to buy all the drinks. I was ready to go for dinner.

George said; "You have time for another."

The times I gave way and had another, but this time I had to go. I had a strict nursing sister at home. Altogether a lovely weekend.

At night, I went to tell my parents they had another grandchild, but they had seven already.

The impression people get of a miner, especially in the city, is a tough looking ignorant all-muscles loud-mouth. But if you really know these miners, some are very good gardeners (winning silver cups) and I have seen some good paintings done by them. I once worked with Tommy Lee who could crochet bed spreads. Some have become M.Ps. They are very kind caring people, excellent family men.

I find, as I go back in my memory, now I am at this stage, all I can write about is mostly work. Because, as a working man, nearly all my life was lived at work. So the next few pages will be about mining.

I first walked to Bestwood pit bottom underground from Calverton shaft No 1 pit bottom. As a miner now at Bestwood pit, I stepped off the cage half way down the shaft at High Main Seam to work. I often hear people say miners dig coal. They don't. They shovel it on to a moving belt. Coal is not just a heap in the ground like soil.

Mother nature puts it in layers, compressed between rock: layers between six inches to six feet. The one at Bestwood was about three feet thick. Imagine looking at a large sponge cake, with a thick layer of cream between the sponge layers. Well, coal is like the cream, but it is between rock. If you tried to take the cream out of the cake, the top half would drop. So the miners taking the coal out of the rock have to hold the rock above them.

On a coal face, this is called the roof. By setting pit props to hold up the roof to get further coal, he works on his knees. The seam, three foot, is about the height of your dining room table.

The face under the rock is a tunnel two hundred yards long. It comes out to a roadway where the rock above has been taken so you can stand up.

Along this tunnel at the coal face are miners every ten yards, throwing coal on to a belt running along the face, to empty itself on to another belt travelling to the pit bottom, then pouring the coal into tubs to go on to the cage.

Each miner on the coal face has a 'stint'. This is the coal he has to get. It is ten yards long. It is cut under the five foot deep coal seam to the length of the Stint. As he gets a yard of coal, he sets a steel prop to hold a long steel bar. This holds the roof, so he can get another yard in. All the miners do this along the face. The face advances as each miner on this Stint threw ten yards, seventeen tons, on the belt. The face is now held up with rows of steel props ready to advance on the next shift.

After my training, I was to start a Stint on Five's face. The routine was, arise at five thirty, pack my snap in a tin, clean towel and soap all in a haversack and walk with the other miners to catch the bus. 'Last cigarette,' leave my clothes in a locker, take a cig and a match, put on working clothes, fill my water bottle with two pints. To the lamp room, pick up my cap light and battery, fasten on my belt, put the lamp on my helmet.

Take my brass check number 1473, put it in my pocket. Sit in the pit yard ready to go down, light the cig as men slowly make their way to the headstocks.

I call in the Powder Mag for a cylinder rubber bag of explosives. You get a shilling for taking one down with you. As the cage comes up, ten men get off, then ten replace them. The cage rises to the next deck, ten get off and ten get on. The cage goes down at speed, twenty men going to work. On the other cage, twenty men coming up from work.

Aproximately fifteen hundred men go down each shift. It is an underground factory. Pit bottom is a hive of activity. Men off the cage go to the Deputies to be sent to their stations. The roads are as high as your lounge. There are trains pulling tubs and to take the miners some two miles or so to the face. Main roads are held up by arched curved iron girders. Diesel trains with open top carriages like you see at the seaside are full of men going to get coal. Then off the trains and walk down smaller roads to the face.

There are men coming off night shift waiting for the train.

They say "What's the weather like?" or "How did Forest go on last night?" That's the local football team. It's like an underground town, a main road with streets coming off it.

At the coal face, you strip off to your waist and put knee pads on for these are to be your shoes on the knees. You now crawl along the face to your numbered ten yards. Sitting on your boots, you put your water bottle and snap tin back out of the way in the gobbins where the coal had been taken, scratch among the dirt to find tools hidden at the finish of the last shift: a large shovel with a short handle because of the height, a sharp pick, a hammer, and a ringer, a steel bar for prising the coal down.

As you move your head, your light follows. Looking along the tunnel in the blackness, lights are like glow worms flitting about. In front of you are the black diamonds you are going to shovel on to the belt.

Along this dark tunnel, twenty-five miners are spaced out, each with their Stint, this three foot layer of coal which has been cut along the floor by a coal cutter, a machine with a five foot steel arm bristling with small picks to cut under the seam. This is done on the night shifts, leaving the coal stuck to the roof.

The miner now clears the coal slack from under his Stint, this long black ten yard coffin of coal hanging from the roof. Another miner has to start to bore holes into the coal. His boring machine is made of alloy for lightness and fixed to a drill four foot long. This is attached to three hundred yards of thick electric cable. Travelling on his knees, he crawls to each Stint drilling four holes to the back of the coal.

Following him is the shotfirer. When he gets to me, I give him the rubber bag of explosives I brought. I help him put sticks of explosive in each hole. After the detonator's in, we couple the wires to thin cables and travel some distance away.

Looking up and down for safety, he shouts: "Firing" and then "Fire" as he turns the key on the battery. There is a dull thud, then the smell of cordite as particles of coal hit your bare back like bee stings.

Going back, all the coal has dropped from the roof. You push the largest lumps on to the belt running on the floor, then shovel a space to the back. This leaves the roof with no support. It looks safe but, at any time, it can fall. You are now covered in sweat, the coal dust sticking to your body, sweat runs down your brow, your eyebrows channel it away from your eyes.

To support the roof, you get a six foot long one inch thick bar of steel (very heavy) and put your hammer, a steel prop and a square of wood ready to go on top of the prop against the bar to stop it slipping.

As you sit on your boots, your helmet touches the roof. Lifting the bar, first on to your shoulder, you space your hands along it and lift it on to your helmet.

You are now a human prop holding the roof up with the bar on your head. Grab the prop and put it under the bar and, with the wood between prop and bar, tap it with your hammer. You are replaced with the steel prop you set. You move away and then hit it up tight. You are now safe and can carry on getting coal.

You get into a rhythm back and forth with the shovel. The belt rides by, loaded as the coal goes down to the other belt and on its way out of the pit.

But it is not always as good. Sometimes the roof comes down with the coal when blasted. So you stand up to look at a cavern with more large lumps of rock ready to come down on you. All the wood you need to shore it up had to come down the belt.

All the miners are getting coal as I have described. When all the coal along the face has gone, it looks like a forest of props, ready to go forward on the next shift. Sitting having snap and a drink, the wooden lids on the props are weeping as the weight above presses down on them. The sap runs down the steel props.

As you eat and drink, the sweat on your body dries with the black dust stuck to it. Although you have done your Stint, and thrown all those tons of coal on to the belt, there maybe someone in difficulties who still has a lot of coal to throw on. You must go down to him and help. One such miner, who was always behind, had the nickname of Riga Mortice, suggesting he had gone stiff.

The air you breathed came from the coal face, so if someone had the call of nature, he dropped his trousers and did it on his shovel, then threw it on the belt. The stench from it drifted in the wind to you and you breathed it in. No toilets. You were back to nature, crawling like animals.

As one chap said "Underground Savages."

The worst thing that could happen was when the roof fell on a miner. All you could see was miners' lights in this long tunnel. To stop the belt loaded with coal you waved your light from side to side relaying it by each miner doing the same until it reached the belt button man to stop the belt.

If a man was buried you waved your beam of light to stop the belt. Then shouting to the miner in the next Stint, by word of mouth down the face, help was called for from the Deputy in charge. If a miner was under a lot of rock, you had to find his head quickly to clear his breathing. In a roof fall, most miners died of suffocation.

Bill and Joan (foreground) with daughter and friends (background) on holiday in Yarmouth.

Probably two miles from the cage, as you cleared the rock someone went for a stretcher and the Deputy would bring morphine (it was kept in a bricked up safe in the wall and the Deputy had a key). The hardest job now was to get him off the face wrapped in blankets on a stretcher. He had to be manhandled down the face, over heaps of coal in a height of only three feet. It was terribly hard work.

If it was only a small injury, you could roll him on the belt and ride out with him with the

157

coal. Out in the road way, you could stand up. Then the stretcher was put on a wheeled trestle to push him along the railway lines.

If there was a serious accident, a doctor would be on his way down if requested by phone to the pit top by the Deputy.

As we stand with him waiting for the train and the doctor, after all the doctor would probably pronounce him dead. Then we would travel with him to carry him to the First Aid room.

Very often a miner was hurt. It would take nearly two hours to get out of the pit. That is why every Deputy and shotfirer was a trained First Aid man.

When the whole length of the coal face for the shift is got, we hide our tools in the dust, pick up our water bottles and snap tins and roll on to the belt like a lump of coal. It will take you out to the train. Into the showers by two o'clock. Two shifts get coal. I had been on day shift, 7.0 a.m. to 2.0 p.m.

Another shift on afternoons, 2.0 p.m. to 10.0 p.m. does as we have done, to take another slice of coal off. Then the night shift, called packers, take down the bars and props left behind and build packs of stones to replace them, moving the belt to the coal face, then cut under the coal again for the next shift.

So the coal face advances, like taking the cream out of the cake a piece at a time.

When you finish work and get out of the cage, the onsetter takes your brass check. That makes sure you have not been left in the mine.

1960

Now in my new job, I could have the weekend off. My daughter was growing up. It was surprising how fast life went by. I spent a lot of time in my garden. The old lady, Mrs Reid, who owned it died. The land was left to a builder.

The new owner told me I could rent another garden at the side of mine, so I now had fowls and ducks and some bantam fowls. These used to lay eggs in secret nests in the orchard to hatch out. Then you would be surprised to see a hen come back with a brood of pheasant-like chicks.

My daughter used to play with her friends among the fowl and ducks: all this nature around with crayfish and trout and shrews on the bank of the stream. After throwing all that coal on each day, I must have had a lot of energy to go digging gardens.

I also bought three geese off a character called Alan. He was about forty, but would not work.

He would say: "Why should I work while all these immigrants are coming to the country drawing money for nothing."

He was a comic. One day he came to the garden. The builder's tip was at the bottom.

He said :"There's a fortune on that tip. Give me a hammer."

He broke old sinks taking the brass and lead out of the base, long copper strips from old shop names and some aluminium kettles and saucepans. He made a big heap on my garden. Taking a kettle, he put half a house brick inside then hammered it in to conceal the brick. As the scrap dealer weighed it, it all made weight. He did the same to saucepans. I was surprised when he gave me five pounds in the local that night: money from the sale of my scrap metal. All the scrap would have been buried. He was a wise man!

My daughter named the geese Dirty, Gerty and Berty. They and the ducks loved it in the stream. They stretched their necks to shout at strangers. I always wore a cap in the garden. I took it off one day and the geese chased me down the garden.

It was near Christmas and they had to go.

I thought: "How do you kill a goose for Christmas?" Their necks are like rubber, but Alan knew. He said you hold the goose with its legs, put a brush stick across its neck, stand on it and pull up to break its neck. I thought what a cruel way, so I left the job to him. I sold two. The other I gave to brother George and his big family.

A long while after, I saw his wife Dot and asked if she liked the goose. She looked puzzled.

"What goose?" she said.

George must have sold it on the way home for beer money. George once told me that the best gardener was the man who came to the garden on Sunday with a bag for a cabbage and a few potatoes and went without paying.

He said a man had done this when he had his garden.

When he asked how much he owed, George said: "Give the kids 10p each." The man put his hand in his pocket.

"How many kids have you got?"

"Fifteen," was the true answer much to the man's surprise.

PET DOGS

One day as I walked down the road with Pamela, Bill Martin spoke to us.

"Come and see our puppies," he said. Six lovely little innocent ones lay in the hearth by the fire. Pamela picked one up and asked if she could have one. He gave it to her.

When we arrived home with it, Mother said :"No." But after tears, she gave way. As it grew up, it was one of the family, a bull terrier. It was a powerful dog. I tried to train it to heel. but it could pull like an express train.

Its appetite was unbelievable. My daughter gave it lots of bananas and it ate the skins. I came downstairs one morning and it had eaten a yard of the lino, no trace of it. I had to cut a square from under the carpet to replace it to keep the peace and quiet.

Its name was Brandy. One day after heavy snow, Pamela was sledging in the lane. I hooked Brandy to the sledge and he was off like a shot. But he died young. I think he was overfed. Tears for a week or two.

Then Grandad bought her a tiny poodle, a small black bundle of fluff, six weeks old. We were advised to feed it on baby milk for a few weeks. I was told to call at the chemists on my way home from work to get some Ostermilk to feed it. In the chemist's shop was 'Hilda,' well-known as the local gossip. She looked at me as I asked for the baby milk. Outside she came to me.

"Got an addition to the family then?" she said.

"Oh yes," I said "It's a lovely little black lad."

With surprise, she said: "Have you adopted then?" I said no, its our new dog. We called this one Tammy. He was a very intelligent dog as I was to find out.

Pamela, now a teenager, was too busy with friends to take him for a run.

As every night I went to the local about nine, the saying was now: "Take the dog with you for a run."

So I took him to the Red Lion pub, my local, where he stayed with me until I came out. In the pub, he was well behaved and was to be a regular like me. He sat on the same form, with his paws crossed. He was treated to chocolate. Most week nights, I drank three pints, then home.

But on a Friday night if I had finished work for the week, I would have an extra pint. But I didn't reckon with Tammy. Now on my third pint, he would sit up and start singing and growling. It was time to go home.

But, when the wife was with me, he never made the Time Please Song. I could drink all night.

He was such a lovely pet and Mother's favourite. He would have the best steak but I would have sausage. He could play hide and seek like a child, find something then go and hide it again.

With the heavy work on the coal face, I lost a lot of weight. I noticed I looked pale and drawn but I was fit with the constant excercise.

Visiting my parents on one occasion, my Father looked very ill. He could not keep his food or drink down. I knew in my mind he had cancer.

Every time I visited him now, he hadn't shaved or washed. I went regular now to shave and.cut his hair and give him a wash. It was a pity to see him like this after his hard working life. He had been so happy in his own way, with a bottle of beer and his pipe and black twist baccy.

As I expected, I was soon visiting him in hospital, at first in a pleasant ward. Then he was moved to a long dismal room. All the beds had very sick people in. I knew this was a ward of no return.

As I propped him up on his pillows, he said: "I want a smoke."

I filled his pipe and lit it, puffing it ready for him, but he did not have breath for it. Tears rolled down his cheeks.

"Bill," he said as he took my hand: "take me home, I want to die in my arm chair by the fire."

He tried to get up but fell back. I left him as tears rolled down my cheeks.

Next day, a phone message. He had died peacefully in the night, but I think someone helped him to die to stop his suffering. He had worked over sixty years. I thought of the years of struggle when we were kids. He was eighty-four. He had been a marvellous Dad.

Mother seemed to get over his death quickly, because she still had the two boys, Melvin and Jeffrey. They were about ten and eleven years now. Mother sent Jeffrey up to my garden every Saturday. She told him he had to learn gardening. She was doing the same as when we were small, teaching things about life. I used to give him five shillings and some produce. He learnt how to dig and sow.

Slowly, television was now coming into people's homes. Cinemas were closing.

When I am now out shopping in Bulwell in Woolworths, I stand and look up at the suspended ceiling. It was once that wonderful music hall. Above was the balcony and, at the end (now a storeroom) was the stage where as a boy I had watched Maria Martin.

Wilkinsons Store up the main precinct: another false ceiling. Above it the high ceiling and the silver screen at the end. As I stand there with my mind in the past, I can hear the old piano with the fat lady thumping as the villain comes on screen.

Further up the main shopping area was the Adelphi Cinema where as a young lad of seventeen we used to queue with a girlfriend, and the commissionaire shouting: "Two seats on the back row in the two and nine's."

But now it's a Bingo Hall. What lovely memories! How life has altered. Sometimes, it seems I have lived a hundred years. In those days, although wages were low, things were very cheap. At eighteen with pals in the pub, I tried my first pint of beer. It was sixpence, or a silver tankard (a half pint) three old pence. Now a pint is £1.30p. I think at the rate things keep rising, there has got to be a halt: go back to prices sixty years ago and start again!

When I tell the tales of how cheap things were, my two grandaughters say: "Don't get the violin out again Grandad. We know about going to Nottingham on a night out with half-a-crown, going to the theatre, having fish and chips and coming home with some change." But I'm jumping forward in time.

NEIGHBOURS DIE

We were the youngest family, in this row of four houses and its communal yard. The other three were all pensioners of my Mother's and Dad's time. At the end, Frank and Anna, around seventy and with no family ties. Then Mrs Grungle, a widow in her seventies.

Next door to us, George and Mary, with a spinster daughter Emma. George had just retired from the pits. All the old people had seen hard times of the twenties and thirties. I listened to them. They were reasonably well off having worked hard from the end of the war.

But why were they afraid to spend their money now in their twilight years? I noticed this fear in a lot of retired people. They didn't like spending the nest egg. What were they saving for?

I did a lot of odd jobs, making cupboards, or boxing in old sinks, putting small fences around their gardens, but they begrudged spending. I think it was from those early days of having to scrat and scrape.

George next door found his wife dead in bed. He went to pieces after. One day I saw him leaning on the gate. I said: "Are you alright George?"

He said: "I miss Mary. I wish I could die to be with her."

He once told me he had enough money to buy a bungalow. Now he wanted to die to be with his wife. He could have gone with his daughter on a cruise, or built a nice place to enjoy his retirement.

The other old people were the same. They never went on holiday. When I tried to make things to improve their living conditions, they were afraid to spend.

166

One Sunday morning at six o'clock, there was a banging on my bedroom wall. I came downstairs. Emma was in the the yard.

"I have been in Dad's bedroom with his morning tea. And I can't wake him up," she said.

She followed me upstairs. It was an old fashioned Victorian bedroom, a large jug and bowl on a wash stand for washing, the large wrought iron bed with brass knobs and ornaments. George lay on it his arms folded across the chest, his mouth wide open. I knew from experience, he was dead. God had granted his last wish. He was with Mary.

Emma burst into tears. I covered his face with a sheet. Downstairs I made some tea, and phoned the ambulance. When it came with a doctor, George was pronounced dead. I had worked with one of the ambulance men, Eddie, in the pit.

A black van pulled up. A knock.

Two solemn men said: "Where's the body?" One went upstairs. The other, with note pad, sat down.

"Do you feel like telling me some details?" he said.

I thought this was a bit quick. He asked how many cars, what price and what type of coffin. Then he asked if her dad had left any special requests.

I was surprised when Emma said: "Yes. He always said he wanted to be buried in his best suit, white shirt, with his cravat on the neck. But no shoes. He said when the last trumpet blows he wants to run free."

What some people believe in!

They couldn't get the box through the door. A large oak dresser that reached the ceiling would not let the door open. So they put him in a body bag and squeezed him round the door to put him in the van. Emma fetched his suit and shirt to go with him. But one man came back.

"Could I have his false teeth? We want him to be properly dressed." It was now ten o'clock. I took Emma to my wife and daughter. She would stay with us for dinner.

What an ordeal.

Frank from the end came in and said: "Come with me and have a pint."

As we passed his house, Anna said: "What a good way to go. No suffering. I hope God takes me the same."

I left Frank in the pub. It was one o'clock.

He said: "I don't go home till two."

We sat round the table, Emma, my wife and Pamela. We talked about her mother and father and what plans she had. She said she would carry on after the funeral and would we attend as she had no relatives. Then came a bang on the door. It was Frank.

He looked at me and said: "It's Anna. She's fallen down in the kitchen. I can't wake her up." We sat him down. I went to look. Emma followed me.

As I entered his back door, Anna lay full length across the hearth in front of the fire. I sent Emma to phone for help. As I turned Anna over, there was a lump on her forehead. I lifted her on the settee. She was dead. I poured a large whiskey from the bottle on the sideboard and sat to wait for the ambulance.

Emma came back. I told her to break the bad news to Frank. It was the same ambulance man, my mate Eddie. He grinned: "Are you on commission?" But, by now, it was like Z cars in the street, two police cars, ambulance and C.I.D. men. They asked me if anyone had broken in. Somebody could have hit her. After looking around, they went. Anna was taken away. I took Frank to his sister up the road.

After the burials, Frank said: "I have been told I can have a flat in sheltered housing, but I think the rent is too expensive."

I said: "You can get help with that from DSS."

"No, you see I have ten thousand in the bank."

I persuaded him to go. Then one day he wanted to take his old carpet to the new flat to save money. He didn't want to spend his nest egg. He died soon after. Some relative from down Cornwall who had never given him a thought or help claimed his money.

Mrs Grungle died in her sleep. Emma stayed in the house with her dad's fortune. But they all had their last wish to die without pain or suffering.

Emma cleared her dad's clothes out. I saw a tweed jacket. She gave it me for work. I took it down the pit. One shift, it dropped off the nail. As I went to pick it up, a five pound note fell out of the top pocket on the floor. George had left me a tip for my help! But he would turn in his grave if he knew.

Now we are in our retirement, we don't like drawing money out of our savings. I wonder why this is?

NEW METHODS IN THE MINE

Coal was the main energy. If there was any stoppage at the pits, it affected the power stations and the whole nation. New machines were being developed to get coal quicker and cheaper. Lots of articles in the papers mentioned AUTOMATION. You never hear that word now.

They said it would put thousands out of work, and urged the Government to build leisure centres to keep these people happy. One example, on the buses the conductors lost their job. You paid the fare to the driver and get a ticket from a machine.Now its called the COMPUTER age.

I was sent to a new coal face and was fascinated at the start of mechanised mining. It's hard to explain. A large space of coal was taken out at the start of the seam and in this space the new machine was assembled. It was powered by a two inch thick pliable rubber electric cable. The machine had cutter jibs, with hundreds of picks on a chain, one to cut at the back, one to cut along the floor and one to cut along the centre of the coal.

As all these picks started cutting, the coal dropped on to a belt as the machine was pulled along the face. Behind, nine miners set props and steel bars to hold up the roof and prevent it falling. As the machine was moving slowly along the coal face, the hundreds of small picks cut the coal.

Two problems! One was the amount of coal dust it made, like a cloud. The other, the large amount of roof it exposed, which could fall on the men.

A chargeman called the Captain was on his knees. He put the heavy steel bars on his shoulders while two of the team set a prop at each end.

170

This was the start of mechanisation. Nine men sent out of the mine two hundred and fifty yards of coal (over five hundred tons) when it had needed thirty men with shovels to equal it.

Within the first months, there were more accidents. One shift, the Captain put a bar on his shoulders up to the roof. But before they could put props under the bar, the roof collapsed on him and he died of suffocation before they could find him.

One afternoon shift, the management agreed that when we had sent out two hundred yards of coal from the pit and made the roof safe we could go home. On one such shift, I started work at two o'clock. We were back home by seven.

My first accident happened when I was setting props behind the machine. It was vibrating the roof and a heavy steel bar dropped down on to my left hand. I looked. My ring finger was pushed into my palm. I had to crawl two hundred yards on my knees to the roadway to see the Deputy. He wrapped it up and sent for a ambulance man to take me out.

At hospital, they put a splint on. I was off work a month, on sick pay, nine pounds a week. I had been earning twenty.

I was on this machine for about two years,. It was named Mecca More. When the machine had cut a face of coal, it had to be dismantled and turned to go back to cut another layer, so at each end it was sent back.

I was told when I went back, I was to work in a stable hole where the machine was turned round. The Mecca More was a success and was ploughing coal out and production went up.

Other machines were being developed that did not need to turn round. It was now like ploughing a field, back and forth.

Without the hardship of the miners shovelling coal, it saved a lot of sweat and toil. And it was turning more coal out of the pit than the miners could ever do. Mechanisation was to close hundreds of mines with overproduction in the future.

Since the accident, my hand was weak and there was loss of grip. So I was off the coal face on light work while I recovered. I was repairing roadways. One good thing: I was off my knees and could walk about. This light work stemmed from private ownwership days. Light work and a lower wage was better than paying full compensation.

Most pits were top heavy with injured men from long past accidents, when they could have left the pit for more suitable work had they been paid compensation.

For example, men who had been told they had dust disease in the lungs were working on roadways still breathing dust in. They should have been paid up and found work in the fresh air.

My new job was to re-widen tunnels supplying the coal face with materials. Mother Nature tried to heal the wounds (i.e. these tunnels) by closing them through the earth's pressure. A roadway six foot high and six foot wide slowly closed so you had to crawl through. My job was to chop them out again.

Have you heard of subsidence? When house doors and windows won't shut properly because the house is tilting. This is caused by the coal face. The earth is in layers called strata. Where the coal has been taken, the stratas break through pressure. Subsidence slowly reaches the foundations of houses causing collapse of the solid ground. Then the house tilts.

One of my mates at work, Jack Baker, was always playing tricks. For example when you went to put your coat on, from hanging on a prop, you would find it nailed to it. In the showers, he would put his hand through into your shower and turn it on to cold water. As I rode home on my push bike struggling to get up the steep hill, he would ride at my side on his small motor bike, tormenting me.

He would say: "Get one of these Crossy." Then he would ride away at speed.

But he died suddenly at fifty-six. I went to the funeral, then later to the house.

To my surprise, his wife said: "I don't know what to do with his Moped. You have always been a pal to him. Would you like it?"

I was very pleased when she said I could have it for £10. A bargain. I rode the Moped all the way home. Then I bought a licence and used it to go to the pit. As it pulled me up the steep hill, I could hear Jack laughing. But I had the last laugh!

Around the time Jack died, quite a few more of my mates died at his age. In my local, I lost four mates that year, all 56. I was pleased when I was 57.

ANOTHER ACCIDENT

Some of the miners I worked with were over seventy. No compulsory retirement age yet. Some of them had been down the pit when I was a boy and when I saw their hardships. I listened to their stories. No safety helmets, just flat caps. No safety boots with steel toecaps, no electric light, just an oil lamp with its tiny light. If it went out it was complete darkness, no chinks of light to guide them. If they had a pony with them, they hung on to its tail to pit bottom, or went down on their knees to follow the small railway lines to a relighting centre to relight the oil lamp.

Under the showers, it was the custom to wash each others' backs to wash the coal dust off. I was amazed at the blue marks like tattoos from cuts that had healed up with coal dust in them, leaving marks like blue cheese. I worked on the coal face with Arthur Parnham aged seventy five. He told me during the war he never saw daylight for months as he worked seven days a week, starting at dawn and coming out when it was dark.

I had done most jobs down a mine, but one day I was told to go and fetch a pony from the stables. The Deputy said we had to move a coal cutter to the face. They are over a ton in weight. At the stables, the ponies were in the stalls. It was Monday morning. I told the hostler what I had to do.

"Take Shilo, " he said "he's the largest, and he's not been out at the weekend."

I could hear him munching. As my light flashed in the stall, mice ran for cover. Perhaps you wonder how they get down a mine? They come down in bales of hay or bags of oats. Then from the pit bottom, they spread all over. I put Shilo's bridle and harness on, hung a large water bottle and bag of oats on it and walked him out of the stables after I put on limmers, light-weight iron shafts, and took a cotter pin to couple to tubs.

We had to travel two miles along the main roads that take the men by train to work. I keep hold of his head. He kicks his heels like a rodeo horse but I calm him down, He now follows behind me. My beam pierces along the high tunnel. When I hear the rattle of chains, it's Shilo getting down on his knees and rolling over and over in the dust. He was like a horse being let out in a field, rolling over for joy. I put him food and water back on, and straighten his harness. He was alright now.

Then, in the distance I could see the light of a train. As it came nearer, I waved my light from side to side. It slowed down. I pushed Shilo into the side and stood by him while the train went slowly by loaded with men

They knew me and shouted jokingly: "Ride him, cow boy," and: "its John Wayne."

We find the coal cutter on the rails on a flat wheeled trolley. Hang up coat, water bottle and food and hook the pony on as he digs in his heels and pulls the coal cutter to the face. From there, it will move on power from the electric cable. We go back and have the snap and a drink. It is near knocking off time so I tie the pony to a prop with his reigns, the leather straps which are used to guide him. Ponies have built-in clocks. He would make his own way home when it was time to go if he wasn't tied up.

I had an apple in my pocket to eat on my way back. I put my hand in my pocket to pull out a handful of pulp. The pony had chewed it in my pocket. I should have known! I walked back the two miles. You were punished by the sack if caught riding a pony. It is a temptation. But ganger's lads have been killed or badly injured by hitting roof girders.

Back in the stables, the hostler examines the pony for injuries. He is put back in the stalls. Some people think pit ponies are blind. This is not true.

I had been back at work after my finger injury for about two months. Four of us were making a stable hole for the coal machine to be pulled into. As I crawled over the belt into the face, a steel roof support was sticking out loose. I pushed it with my right hand.

It tilted and trapped my hand to the roof making a small cut in my right finger. I poured some water on it from my bottle. It was very painful, but I carried on. My hand swelled up. On the train coming out, my pals said it looks like you will have to have it off, joking.

After a shower, I showed it to the first aid man. He said it's deep cut but small. If it gets worse, see the doctor. It was Saturday, doctor was closed. By Monday, my hand was badly swollen. The doctor said I had blood poisoning and gave me a penicillin injection. I was back to work two days later.

A month after, I was in the Mecca More stable hole, the machine was on its way towards us cutting coal. I reached out for my shovel. As I grasped the handle, there was a sharp pain in my middle finger and a click. The pain went. But as I shovelled, my finger would not bend around the handle. I carried on, but after a shower I saw the first aid man. He told me to see a doctor.

The doctor told me the tendon in my finger was damaged by the deep cut of the old injury and now it had snapped. He gave me a letter to see a surgeon at the General Hospital, Mr.Burkett. He told me that pieces of gristle in my fingers work them like puppets on a string. One had broken.

He could repair it by taking a small tendon from my wrist to replace the broken one. He said there is a spare tendon there. He said I would have to be in a week, but it was the annual holidays and I had booked for Yarmouth.

I went in after my holiday.

HOSPITAL

I was admitted to a ward. My arm was shaved and painted with iodine and put in a sling.

Next morning at ten o'clock, I was taken to the theatre. I had my arms folded over my chest. I next remember coming round. It was three o'clock by the ward clock. A white lump was hanging near my head. I had a feeling my arms were still folded. But I looked and it was my arm in plaster to the elbow.

My feet were burning and hot. I asked the nurse to take off my bedsocks. They were hot and uncomfortable.

She lifted the bed clothes and said: "You have had an operation on your foot."

When my wife came, she laughed and said: "Perhaps you fell out of bed."

The surgeon, Mr Burkett, said: "I'm sorry. We cut your arm but the tendon wasn't suitable. So we took one out of your foot."

Back home, I was hobbling about on a crutch. My pals from the Coopers took me for a drink on a bike sitting on the saddle to push me up there.

In a fortnight, I went in to have the stitches out. It made me feel sick to see what they had done. Nine stitches in my foot. My toes still worked. Thirty stitches in my arm up to my elbow and my finger was bent to my palm.

I had eighteen weeks off work. Still my finger would not move. It was useless. I went back to work on a light job but now the finger was a handicap. It got stuck in my pocket. It kept getting hooked on things at work. I saw Mr Burkett again. It was a shock when he said he wanted me back in hospital again to take a piece out of my other foot and try again. So I insisted I have the finger taken off. He finally agreed. Then he told me that if I lived in Australia, they could have taken a tendon from a kangaroo. They have tendons like ours.

So, I had my finger off and I have never been handicapped. I went back to mining. All those years working a circular saw and I never lost a finger. Now I had one missing. All my working life I never had an accident. Now two within months.

My garden had been a great pleasure to me to keep me occupied while off work. It was Summer time. I stepped over the stream to go for my pint. In the Coopers Arms' orchard near the stables was a pigsty with the largest pig I have ever seen. It had been fed with beer from the bottom of barrels and was always asleep. I suppose it was drunk most of the time.

My garden was full of produce, with the fowls and the ducks laying well.

One day I dipped my kettle in the pure spring water from the brook to make tea, as I often did. Floating by was some brown sausage looking objects from the cottages higher up. Someone had emptied the bed chambers. I felt sick.

Then I thought what the ducks had been eating. What a disgusting thing to do. I took bottles of water to the garden after that.

My Mother, now eighty-four, was very ill. She told me she would have to go into hospital. The two boys were sent back to George and Dot. But, like my Dad, it was a visit of no return.

I had a message at work that she had fallen on getting out of bed and broke her hip. I went to see her.

She told me she had waited two hours for a bed pan in the night. She was forced to get out of bed and slipped on the floor. Within two days, she died. Now they are both at rest in the same grave on the hill.

My wife fetched the clothes from the hospital and the key to the house. I had a letter from the landlord to clear the house. I asked my eldest brother if he wanted anything.

As I put my key in the door, still on the old pine table were the medicines, the teapot, tinned milk, two pot dogs now on the piano, the old black fireplace and the large black kettle now cold and silent.

But, upstairs there were drawers half open and empty. I took a pair of cut glass swans, a thing of beauty still on the shelf. I took them for the memory.

I ordered a van and put what was part of their life of at least sixty years of marriage up to my garden in the big fowl hut. The piano nobody wanted in this age of record players, radio and television. I remember the man coming every Friday night for the instalments.

In 1928 it cost 49 guineas, a fortune in those days. I sat down and played it to the chickens, Chick Chick Chicken, Lay a Little Egg for Me.

The old table was made into nest boxes. What a story that could have told. The glass out of the pictures of my dead relatives was used in the greenhouse. The old pegged rug was put in front of my hut fireplace.

The brass fender and the two large 1914 shell cases and fire irons etc George must have taken to the scrap man for beer money.

The bedsteads filled up gaps in the hedge row.

All their worldly goods.

Now, in a new stage of our life, we were offered a house just down the road by a friend of the family. It was much better but still outside toilets. But we had hot water and a modern fire place but, again, no bath.

DEPRESSING DOWN THE PIT IN SUMMERTIME

At the pit now all the coal faces were mechanised. Some of the new machines had two drum like heads full of small picks, like the comics I had as a child where a machine could travel through the earth boring its way. This new machine, the Trepanner, could plough up and down the coalfield like ploughing a field. The hydraulic roof supports like car jacks could push the roof up.

Where a mine would take a hundred years to clear the coal by shovel, these machines shortened the life of a mine by half. So soon, rumours that the Bestwood pit was to close.

In Summertime, it was depressing to have to go down the pit on afternoons. On day shift, it was up early and away. But afternoon shift and the time waiting to go to work: thank goodness for the pleasure of the garden. As the sun broke through, it was very hot.

I tended my sweet peas and watched the may fly float down the stream breaking out of its cocoon. But before it could get airborne it was gobbled up by a trout. Near the hedge was a Jenny Wren flitting in and out of the ivy. Then the bright colours of the kingfisher with its nest in a hole in the bank of the stream.

All this and thoughts of going down the pit, I decide to have a pint of beer. Over the stream through the orchard, the pig lies in the sun snoring. Its trough is full of beer slops.

In the tap room, Ernie, the landlord, brings me a pint and bangs the dominoes down: "You make four."

I say to the two other miners; "What shift are you on?"

"Afternoons," the grim reply.

Twelve noon I get up to go.

181

"A day like this!" says Ted. "My Stint is sky high. The whole face has collapsed. Some of the falls have left it sixteen foot high and rocks hang there as big as this table. I'll have another pint. I may have a holiday Ernie," said Ted.

I caught my bus at one o'clock. Sitting in the pit yard having my last cigarette waiting to go down the black hole. Now the sun was scorching hot, it was tempting to go back to the garden. But I walked up slowly to the cage.

Next morning, another hot day. The same routine. As I sat down for my usual pint, Ernie didn't bring the dominoes. There was only three of us.

"Where's Ted?"

"Haven't you heard. He went to work after all. He said he needed the money. But there was a massive fall of rock and he was under it. They dug him out dead."

I felt like getting drunk but I needed the money and I went to catch the bus in the brilliant sunshine.

Time after time I thought of finding a fresh job, but a regular wage plus a load of coal each month and I was hooked.

Down the road the local chip shop closed owing to retirement. I thought: "Shall I ask them if I could buy the business." I could have borrowed the money. I deserved better than this with my knowledge and experience.

I remember thinking as I finished my Stint on the coal face on afternoons hundreds of feet underground covered in sweat and coal dust: "Do people who sit in their centrally heated rooms in London know what it takes to keep them warm and comfortable?"

I was getting known as the local odd job man. I could put in a light switch, build a fence, put windows in, make a dog kennel. The old forge (with the joiner and undertaker attached) where I went as a boy was still open. An old employee had been given it by the owner as he had worked for them since he was a boy. Jack Olivant was his name, quietly spoken, a typical undertaker. I met him in the Cross Keys bar. He told me he was very busy and could I help Saturdays.

I did quite a lot of work for him including making coffins. He asked me to work for him but the wage he offered could not match the pit job and the coal for free. It was a pity, a chance to get out of mining and perhaps of going into business.

One job I did for him was to replace some broken window cords in some houses. It's hard to believe how some people live. A scruffy old lady opened the door she said: "The bedroom window, we can't shut it."

I went up the stairs. What a sight! No bedlinen, just two old overcoats on the bed, a bed chamber full to the top and cigarette ends floating on it. I went to take the lace curtains down. They dropped to bits and the room filled with dust. I repaired the cords. As I was coming out, I noticed the bare floorboards were mottled with burn marks. It puzzled me what they were. On my bike coming home, I felt dirty. Then it struck me that the burn marks were from someone laying in bed lighting a cigarette and throwing the lighted match on the floor. I thought of when I was young, of the slums which were never so bad. But this was 1964 and people lived like this.

My daughter was now eleven. She was always in the garden with friends. I made a swing on the apple trees. One day, as she fed the fowls she pointed out one as being ill. It was crop bound. When a fowl eats, the food goes into a bag on its chest, then is digested from there. This fowl had eaten a lot of dried grass, making a large ball it could not get rid of.

Not thinking, I said: "It will have to be killed."

She cried: "No. Don't kill it Dad." After a while, I went to the library to read about poultry ailments. I asked Pamela to help me operate on the fowl. As she held it down on the table, I followed the book, plucked the feathers off its chest. With a razor blade, I cut the skin which was puffed up like a ball, avoiding blood vessels. We pulled all the straw, like a bird's nest, out. Then with a needle and white thread, we sewed it up. Pamela jumped for joy as it ran to join the others.

Next day she said: "It's on the nest, Dad." We could tell it by its bare chest. And it carried on to lay eggs. She called me Doctor Cross after this life-saving act.

Our new abode was a much larger house and a more refined area, but I still went up to the Coopers. It was good company. The landlord, Ernie, had not been well.

He called me over and said: "Do you want some fowl muck for your onions?" I said yes.

"Well, go into my poultry hut. It is three inches deep," he said. I went and cleared it all by barrow and wheeled it over the brook to my garden. I went back thinking he might buy me a drink, but he said: "When you go back, Bill, throw some lime powder along the perches and boards." It suddenly hit me. I had cleared his fowl house out and disinfected it with lime. What a character! Next time I went in he gave me a sly grin.

He said: "There's an old barrow leaning against the wall in the orchard. You can take it for your garden." As I went through, I wheeled it to the stream. It completely dropped to bits. The wheel rolled into the brook. I cursed him. He was getting rid of his rubbish.

It was Goose Fair when one night I was drinking with the boys in the Coopers when Joe Evans came in with a pomegranate from the Fair. Someone said you can't grow them in England.

Joe said: "I bet Bill can." Someone bet half a crown.

So for fun I told Joe I would grow one. Every night, he asked me if it was growing. So I bought a pomegranate from a local shop, broke a stem off a laurel bush and pushing a stem into the fruit planted it tight in a plant pot for a bit of a lark. Joe was thrilled with it and, to my surprise, won his bet of half a crown. The following night I asked Joe what he had done with the plant.

"My lad, Ken, took it to school. The teacher has put it in the window," he said. We never told Joe it was a fake. I wonder if he found out it wasn't real?

George Stevens, a local miner, asked one night: "Do you want any pork?" I said: "Yes, I'd have a joint for Sunday dinner." I went to his cottage near the quarry. I knocked and he shouted: "Come in." I was surprised. Across his kitchen table was a complete pig. He was scrubbing it with hot water and a brush.

"How much do you want?" asked George.

"A piece about one pound in money." He took a sharp knife and cut off one of its back legs, trotter included. "Give me thirty bob," he said. "Do you listen to the Archers? I shall write to them to tell them about that pig's illness. The vet got it wrong. I might go down in the van and give them advice." He thought the programme was real. I left with a leg on my shoulder. I got a bargain.

PART 6

ADAPT AGAIN

At fifteen, my daughter was thinking of going to college to be a children's nurse. I seem to think that with being an only child, she wanted to look after children. My sister-in-law, her Aunty Mavis, was like a second mother to her, taking her on trips and holidays.

The wife's mother died at fifty-six. She had been a hard working woman like my Mother. She had seen very hard times with her husband a miner in the struggle in the thirties. It was a terrible shock to the family her dying so young.

I now had another shock from a special delivery letter I had to sign for. It said the Council had put a Compulsory Purchase Order on the land of my garden. I was to be off it in one month.

There was to be a slum clearance of the whole area where I lived. I quickly had to sell off the ducks and fowl. My garden was full of produce. It was a shame.

Within five weeks, the bulldozer made a way through the greenhouses and fowl huts, for a main sewer. The brook with all its wildlife was diverted into a sewer.

Then, this lovely community was destroyed as they sent people to live miles away.

Those people in planning offices probably never left their chairs to destroy people's lives.

With a bit of thought, they could have knocked down a small area, built new houses and moved people in relays to keep them in the same environment and families.

Now, as I went to the Coopers Arm, it reminded me of the London blitz. Just the pub left standing. A letter came one morning with thirty pounds compensation for loss of my garden. I had just moved to this house, or I should have had to go far away because my cottage, where I lived before, had now gone.

I applied to a rent tribunal about the rise in rent. They were knocking down houses with bathrooms. The official who came told me by Act of Parliament I was entitled to better living conditions.

So I made an appointment to see my M.P. Nobody seemed to bother about our living conditions. I told him I wasn't racist but I did not think it fair that coloured people were moving into modern homes. I was a British subject like them. I had been through the war etc. He said he would look into it.

A Council man from the rent office came to see me. He said I had caused trouble by seeing my M.P. They were going to make the small bedrooms of the row of houses into bathrooms. That would make them one-bedroom tenancies.

But where my garden had been, it was a new road with nice new houses still in the terrace design. A friend who had one asked me to look around his new house. I decided I should like one.

My wife, Joan, had a part-time-job. We were still trying for a house with a bathroom.

In this year 1968, we were still using the tin bath.

We were told Bestwood pit was closing. The miners would be sent to work in other pits. I decided to find a job out of the mines. I had an interview for a school caretaker. I got the job but I was to move into a school house in Nottingham. My wife did not want that.

I was now aged fifty: as Pamela said half a century. I saw a job in the local paper for a machinist and sawyer. It was at Flewitt's in Basford. I was lucky. I saw the owner. He showed me the machines. I told him I had been at the pit for twenty years.

Then he said: "Where did you learn the trade?"

I said: "Hopewell's in Basford."

He said: "That's good enough for me if you worked there. It's like riding a bike or learning to swim, you never forget a trade." I had the job. I put my notice in at Bestwood pit.

On the first day, I sharpened a saw just as if I had never been away. It was strange working in daylight and fresh air, a cup of tea and a smoke, after all that time underground. It was that interesting, sawing and planing and the lovely smells of pine. I was worse off for money and now I had to buy coal.

But I was back to a life I enjoyed. I was very happy in my new work setting machines to make floorboards, skirting boards and mouldings for builders. We were very busy on contracts for Wimpeys. In my tool shop, I had made a small lathe, I had all my joiner's tools. Lunch times I spent making small items of furniture. I used the hard wood from crates. It was an easy going firm.

Now I was annoyed at the Council for doing nothing about the bathroom situation. I went to see my M.P. again. He tried to put me off with more excuses. I told him I was prepared to go on TV showing me sitting in the tin bath in this day and age.

He said: "Oh, don't do that!" Next day, a housing official came. He gave me the address of a house and said I should look at it. I would have the chance of others. I was surprised it was near the Coopers Arms at the side of my old garden. But it would be three months before we could move in because the tenants were buying a house and it wasn't ready.

Pamela had been courting for over a year. Now they saw a house to buy and decided on the wedding day, July 20th 1973. They had a better start to marriage than I did. It was a lovely wedding with about one hundred guests. But it wasn't very nice when guests asked to go to the 'bathroom' and it was the outside toilet.

Bill and his daughter arriving at Bulwell Parish Church

We were back to the beginning on our own waiting for our new house. Our lives have moved in a complete circle back to where we used to live and back to work in a timber yard as I did a long time ago.

My eldest brother died. I had been helping him with his allotment as it was getting too much as he was over eighty. He had been in his garden the day before he died. The best way to go. This left me and my younger sister. We didn't keep in touch. My brother left me the allotment and all the digging. Then it was too much for me. It was near the Coopers and where I lived.

After I left the pit, they made thousands of miners redundant and paid them a nest egg. I missed out on that. Then the timber firm closed a year after I retired.

Bill, Joan and Pamela in York.

The men I had worked with received thousands of pounds. I missed out because they don't pay after retirement, so I have never had a lot of money.

I have now finished work for over ten years from the timber trade. After being a soldier and a miner, I come back full circle in my life. I think with this record of past events, I have left my mark.

After leaving work, my source of small pieces of hard wood from which I used to make small items of furniture stopped. To buy this wood was too expensive. But on walks around country lanes I found things people had dumped. I found a small oak table, its legs broken, thrown into the hedgerow.

In my workshop, I stripped the varnish off with paint stripper and recycled it into a small wine table. This gave me the idea of recycling old wood.

The furniture we had bought nearly fifty years ago was to be replaced by modern, starting with buying a white wardrobe made from man-made wood, 'contiboard.'

So I took the old oak wardrobe to pieces and had plenty of suitable wood.

For years I wanted a reproduction grandfather clock. Copying from an old drawing, I turned the wardrobe into a battery operated chiming clock (see photo on next page). It gave the old wood a new lease of life perhaps for another fifty years.

I have left memories of the past in the base of the clock. I put the daily paper and small items of interest to be found when the last chime strikes and it is broken up. I have done this with other things I have made. Our old pre-war furniture has all been

Bill with his grandfather clock, 1995.
Photo: Michael Penty

recycled into useful furniture for the future.

My family come to tea on Sunday. But I make sandwiches and we sit around the telly. I think of the teas my Mother made. My granddaughters are now teenagers. How time flies. I still like to talk of the past.

As I write this, I appreciate life today with central heating, electric light, television and the bathroom we always wanted.

I still go for a pint of beer but stopped smoking fifteen years ago. What a waste of money all those years. I remember all this past, but now I go shopping with a list like a little boy because I forget things. I have a go on the Lottery. What would I do with the money if I won it?

I have been on the pools thirty years: never won! Will my luck change?

Today is Valentine's Day. The room is full of greeting cards.

Forty seven years of marriage. My daughter's birthday. So this is the end of my story but not my life. I love to go out for a meal in a nice hotel. It's grand to be alive, so we will celebrate. I am pleased I recorded these events.

As I sit here typing with all the mis-spelt words, I enjoy it very much. I can thank my two granddaughters for the gift of the typewriter. I have been in hospital. I have had a very active life. I have been told to sit and rest so I am typing and sitting.

This lovely warm room fitted with carpets, cosy chair, gas fire. October 1994.

We do have a good life today. I appreciate the modern life, but today's generation don't know any other. At the touch of a light

194

switch the room is lit up. Think of the paraffin lamp. Turn a knob and the fire throws out warmth. Think of chopping sticks and trying to get a fire to boil water.

I can see my Father now at the black fireplace and a few sticks burning in the grate, and a small saucepan of water to boil to make us a cup of tea before we went to work. No other means to boil water.

Press a switch and see pictures of what's going on around the world and films in your own living room. No Monday washdays which lasted three days. Switch on, set a programme and your washing ready to iron in less than one hour!

It seems impossible in seventy years the advances that have been made. What will it be like in another seventy years?

Or will this world be destroyed by man himself?

SOME WAYS YOU CAN HELP CREATE COMMUNITY HISTORY

*** RUTH'S ARCHIVE

Ruth I Johns, Editor of this series, has started a much needed archive of community activity. RUTH'S ARCHIVE offers you an opportunity to write your own account of your experiences in a user-friendly fill-in book which, when completed, you return to the Archive for safe keeping.

RUTH'S ARCHIVE will become a public resource for study from around the year 2000. Future generations will get an opportunity to hear your voice and not only the voice of the 'experts.'

Too often history is written about us and not by us.

MY HISTORY OF COMMUNITY ACTIVITY is printed on 40 pages of archive quality paper which will last at least 500 years. The book has an introduction and enough structure to help you in your task (which people always say they enjoy once they get started).

There is no 'correct' way of filling in the book. You are free to do it in any way and style you wish. For some people, it is the first time they have written anything bigger than a greetings card for some years!

Many people have already sent in their completed books. They have found the experience of writing about their lives fun as well as thought-provoking and very satisfying. Older people often comment that filling in their book has helped them to see that they have achieved much more than they thought.

This is because the book seeks your experiences not only of major events but also of those very important, usually unrecorded, smaller ones which people often undertake without fuss or recognition: things which are the building blocks within any community.

It is urgent that we place on record the happenings, the people and the ideas which have been important to us. How else will future generations have any idea of how life has been lived in real communities?

RUTH'S ARCHIVE started in Nottingham but is now open to **anyone living in the U.K**. Here are a few comments about the Archive from the many people who are welcoming it:-

*** *"RUTH'S ARCHIVE should fill a major gap in the official record."* Adrian Henstock, Principal Archivist, Nottinghamshire Archives.

*** *"For many years, my activities outside my work have been to do with my large family, including sixteen grandchildren, who mostly live nearby."* Alice Griffin, Warwick.

*** *"So much of the ordinary, everyday activities and events of people's lives never get recorded, and yet this is the very basis of social history... Only by understanding the interwoven contributions of individuals to a community do we begin to get a clear picture of what that community was."* Corinne Phillips, Local Studies Library, Chapel Bar, Nottingham.

*** "*I was well looked after in the City Hospital and I promised myself to put back into the community the good care I received at that hospital in 1955.*" Pearl Hands, Meadows.

*** "*Over and over again people have come up with new ways to improve life in their area, and with time and effort demonstrated that they work. All too often this is when the powers-that-be step in with money or professionals to take over and take all the credit, I hope RUTH'S ARCHIVE is an opportunity for those who are usually forgotten to put things from their point of view, and show the extent of their achievements.*" Colin Haynes, Sneinton.

*** "*I have been involved with community work since being a child of nine and have found great satisfaction in helping others. I think the story of community work should be told.*" Violet Dixon, Bestwood.

*** "*When the histories of our time get written up, they rarely give voice or place to the lives of ordinary people. To put together this ARCHIVE of how history was experienced 'on the streets' could be one of the richest legacies we could leave to future generations who must make sense of the times we have lived through.*" Alan Simpson, MP.

Send £6 to obtain your own copy of
MY HISTORY OF COMMUNITY ACTIVITY
to
RUTH'S ARCHIVE,
P.O. Box 66,
Warwick CV34 4XE.

Or buy one to send as a gift to an elder person who is special to you.

198

*** PLOWRIGHT PRESS invites you to send in your written account of your personal experience of any of the following:-

1) "MY EXPERIENCE OF LIVING IN A MINING COMMUNITY."

Whether you were/are a miner, a woman in a mining community or a child growing up in one, tell us about the experiences which are/were especially important for you. Or describe your everyday life, or a particular event...

Please give as much detail as possible and always state the place and dates about which your write.

Write up to 20 sheets of paper

2) "THE PLACE I HAVE MOST ENJOYED LIVING IN."

Describe in as much detail as possible the place in which you have most enjoyed living. Where? When? Why? How old were you?

Write up to 20 sheets of paper

3) "MY EXPERIENCE OF SETTLING IN BRITAIN AS AN IMMIGRANT."

Where did you come from? Why did you come? Decribe in as much detail as possible your experiences of your first few years here. If you would like to tell your life story including the time before you came and your subsequent experiences once you settled here, please do.

Write any length

Your writing on any of these experiences will be considered for publication.

Please write using a word processor, typewriter or clear handwriting. Express your experiences in any style you wish.

When writing, give accurate and detailed descriptions and avoid generalisations and a false sense of nostalgia.

Tell things the way they were/are. Remember to give place names and dates when appropriate.

Send to PLOWRIGHT PRESS,
P.O.Box 66,
Warwick CV34 4XE.

Enclose a stamped addressed envelope if you want acknowledgement of the safe arrival of your writing. You will be contacted if your contribution can be used for publication. We will use as many contributions as publication costs allow.